THE COMPLEAT FLEA

THE COMPLEAT FLEA

Brendan Lehane

THE VIKING PRESS

NEW YORK

FOR JUDY

Published in 1969 by The Viking Press, Inc.
625 Madison Avenue, New York, N.Y. 10022

Library of Congress catalog card number: 69-12251

Printed in Great Britain

CONTENTS

ILLUSTRATIONS

ILLUSTRATIONS

AUTHOR'S NOTE

I am very grateful to Mr F. G. A. M. Smit, Custodian of the Flea Department at Tring, for giving me so much time and kind advice, and for a highly corrective reading of the type-script. I am also indebted to the Hon. Miriam Rothschild for sending me several of her published and unpublished papers and giving me good advice in letters; her very readable book *Fleas, Flukes and Cuckoos* was also of great use. For help in various ways I want to thank Dr D. A. Humphries who sent me papers on his work of which I took full advantage; Mrs Lynn Wright who kindly read the typescript and made many corrections; Miss Cecily Baker of the Charles Van Pelt Library, University of Pennsylvania; Mrs Fiona Cowell; Mr Henry Ford; Mr Peter Fryer; Mr David Hughes; the ever-courteous staff of the British Museum Library; and far from least my wife Judy. Again I am most grateful to Mrs Osyth Leeston, Mr Marshall Best and Mr John Murray for all their advice and encouragement.

'While ruder heads stand amazed at those prodigious pieces of nature, as Elephants, Dromidaries, and Camels; These I confesse, are the Colossus and Majestick pieces of her hand; but in these narrow Engines there is more curious Mathe⁄maticks, and the civility of these little Citizens, more nearly sets forth the wisdome of their Makers.'

SIR THOMAS BROWNE *Religio Medici* 1642

INTRODUCTION

It was February when I took a ground-floor flat in Dublin.
I was in love with old Ireland, and came to the place to do my
researches on the Celts. The flat had more rooms than I could
use and was very cheap. The bus that passed nearby took me
close to the National Library. I knew no difference between
lice and fleas. My concern was kings and saints, Cuchulain
and Columba, Deirdre, the O'Neills and Tara. After a
week I wrote in my diary:

> The flat has many insects in it, though lots are dead through
> spreading powders. I have a good twenty flea bites, or so I
> imagine them. The worst is all the carcases of woodlice and
> silver-fish round the walls that I clear up daily. They are
> white and dry and I imagine the powder burns them.

But I was loving my stay in Dublin. The cool wind blew
roses into the cheeks of girls and there were twenty minutes
listening to poetic blarney before you could buy a pound of
butter. The streets were wide and all the doors of the Georgian
houses were differently painted and had lintels and pediments
of individual design. A month later I wrote in my diary:

> Insect life reveals itself more. I don't want to dwell on it for
> fear of an obsession but I've seen three maggots, quarter of
> an inch long or more and plump, two under the bookcase
> and one giving a spider, on whose web it was caught, an
> apparently insoluble problem. No fleas for a few days but
> this assault with powder and spray will probably bring
> them out. I'm aware of tickles all over my body which I
> mightn't otherwise register. I can't help marvelling at fleas.
> Their back legs are as long as their bodies, for jumping;

kangaroos of the insect world. I read they can jump eighty
times their own height. This objectivity is a bit of a pose.
I'm getting squeamish.

Squeamish I was. The flat was cheap, but nothing had
been said about sharing with an inimical species. I mentioned it to the landlord, but in an off-hand way, for fear he
should think the fleas arrived with me. He embellished a sly
manner with an ocular twinkle. We were soon talking of
London and I was glad to drop the subject.

I continued to record my reactions in the matter of insects.
At night I whisked the bedclothes back and examined along
the tucks. I turned my clothes inside out and brushed them
down, especially the seams. I discovered to my dismay that
life was full of tiny black things. I swatted crumbs of toast and
innocuous specks of dust. With Vaseline-coated fingers I made
cautious assaults on minute fragments of bark and twig that
the breeze blew in. The tawny matting of my flat was dappled
white with poisonous powders. Itching marred my enjoyment
of the gentle eloquence of the Irish shopkeeper and of an evening of Michael Mac Liammoir, playing Yeats at the Gaiety
Theatre. I knew the meaning of nerves. Maeve and Con-
chobar and the Red Branch knights meant less to me than
those little people with whom I had become perforce familiar.
By April my diary was coming on better than my Irish book.
I wrote:

> I use Vaseline to pick up fleas I find. 'They are immobilised
> and one can look at them closely and safely. Erica used to
> crack them between her nails, but I've never managed that
> and don't fancy it. The bathroom, damp and dark, has
> hundreds of little flea-like insects in it that sit on the wall and
> move quite slowly. I destroy them now and again with a
> spray and get bodies over bath and floor. A couple of
> spiders with lateral webs like gummy trampolines get a rare
> old feast all the time. If these insects drop in the bath, and I

turn on the tap to wash them away, they jump just like fleas, though not high enough to escape. They land a little way up the side, then slide back under pressure of a stray drop of water. They go on jumping till caught by the flood. There's a strong resemblance to flies, but the jump is quite distinct from flying. Is the fly proper a later stage of this fly-thing? And did flies ever jump or fleas fly?

I was becoming inquisitive. Along with obsession came the academic appetite. In this respect it was fleas that held my attention. 'Fleas *are* attractive,' I wrote, 'though fondness grows with absence. Other insects haven't the same appeal.' Fleas were so clever at avoiding capture. I could chase and investi-gate, stealthily track, viciously strike, and just in time their lithe mechanisms would eject them to cover. Next morning the tokens of their feast would swell, redden and smart, trophies of victory. They seemed to anticipate my thoughts, to relish the game, as hunting men would have us believe foxes do.

To add to the embarrassment of public scratching, enter-taining guests became an agony. My sister and brother-in-law stayed a weekend at a hotel nearby. In my flat we drank coffee and talked. The first afternoon my sister rested on my bed. Later I was impulsively watching every move of her hands and found it difficult to concentrate. I could not bring myself to explain. On Sunday I noticed my brother-in-law was the victim. His hand moved often to his midriff. I pictured him with twenty bites, as I had been, and the memories he would take away with him. He had once been a commando, though, and never said a word.

Spring bloomed and blossom festooned the streets of Dun-drum and Rathmines and Dartry. Timeless Celts looked down at the timeless Liffey from O'Connell Bridge and the quays, and sometimes spat gobbets of tobacco into the water. One midnight some patriots blew the top off Nelson's column. I took railway tickets to Drogheda and Sligo, climbed Knocknarea, and watched the humped backs of the Ox Mountains swathed in mist, and the table summit of Ben Bulben below which the hosts of the Tuatha slew the hosts of the Fir Bolg, far back in the Celtic dawn. In early May I wrote in my diary:

No fleas for about a fortnight. Then woke this morning to find fresh marks of bites on my right hip, cursed and searched, found nothing. Then bitten on the right ankle, then the left, in spite of a bath and complete change of clothes. Finally I got it. It fell off my left foot as I undressed, and I managed to pick it out, with Vaseline, from the carpet. A small one. It went in its embalming grease to the dustbin. I read that fleas can stay in furniture and clothes for a long time till humans come along and the forced fast stops. Must find out about their breeding, and why they disappear for weeks then return. Must write an article about fleas. Life among the fleas. They are rather elegant with their slim build and hump-backed shape and long powerful back legs. And comic, cunning, self-willed.

Attacks are fewer, in spite of this morning. I must be winning. Most insect life dead. It got me down earlier. I imagined I felt them moving all over me. Amazing about nerves, just like body police. They get information all the time. When one moves a leg it rubs a little against the trouser. Hairs are pulled back, then, released, spring into place like a catapult, tapping the skin. Sometimes it may be blood passing through veins constricted by an awkward position. Normally the nerves file no report. These are routine occurrences. Then there are fleas and it becomes a state of emergency. Everything must be reported. So the brain becomes a sorting house for all these minor alarms, most of which are false. It was exhausting and went on at night too. All those little messages from toes and shins and all the rest.

A mood of relief. I would expect peace for my last few weeks, freed from blight and pest. But victory so far was my Alamein, and there was more war to follow. The day before I left Dublin I wrote in my diary:

> Fleas again. I'm under attack, the day before I leave for good. Will I take them back with me?

I remember the irritation of the hot bumps as I crossed the sea from Ireland, discomfort augmented by the alcoholic miasmata of Irishmen going to dig for gold on England's building sites. On the train from Liverpool to London I scratched again, told myself to forget the itches by not thinking about them, and succeeded only until insidious tingling brought nails to flesh without my conscious mind being informed.

What I had, by this time I suppose, was an obsession, a preoccupation with the minute. In London the obsession was kept alive for a few weeks by the diminishing forays of those fleas that accompanied me, stowing away in my clothes or luggage. Then, as my interest diluted from obsession to curiosity, I found a fascination in those whose experiences led them to a more intense involvement. Plenty exist.

What in my case were suspicions become for them delusions. The toast crumb *is*, for a while, a flea. Assured this is not so, they take it to belong to some other insect genus, beyond scientific knowledge. They go to a doctor. The doctor tells them it is toast. They despair of doctors and seek higher authority. They send sample particles of toast or other matter to hospitals and research institutes. Insomnia, brought on by psychosomatic tickles, tenses their nerves and makes taut their minds. Some researchers have drafted letters to send in reply to all these pleas and packets of inconsequential fragments.

All this preoccupation goes much further in backward parts of Italy, where a curious hysteria is found. There, the bite of the tarantula spider is held to contain a mystic power.

The afflicted can be purified only by dancing, and musicians are hired to charm the evil spirits away. This cleansing—an annual outburst of spasm and frenzy—takes place in churches dedicated to St Paul. Victims dance, musicians in relays play tarantellas, and in time symptoms are allayed and followed by tranquillity. Scientists deny any material con⁄nection between bite and symptoms. Arthropodic make⁄believe it may be, but it can clutch minds and change lives.

I know of no similar treatment for a flea fixation, and it might be worth somebody's trouble to devise one. My own therapy was to examine the experiences of others in every available source. The search ultimately brought me peace of mind. It brought me also a certain friendliness to fleas.

A word on parasites

Almost
All the wise world is little else, in Nature,
But parasites and sub⁄parasites
BEN JONSON

That being so, we tend normally to distinguish only be⁄tween big parasites and little ones, or between human and animal and insect parasites. Little insects are little insects. Mosquitoes are known by their menacing hum, ants by their shape, but the rest remain just insects, or bugs, or crawlies, or even—in a slanderous blurring of generic edges—all fleas. The variety of insect parasites makes this confusion under⁄standable. Spots from the bites of fleas, lice, mosquitoes, bed⁄bugs, midges, ants, horse⁄flies, stable⁄flies, harvest⁄mites, and many others seem much the same and equally unpleasant. Besides, parasites are such a numerous tribe. They get into the oddest places and live on most peculiar diets. One worm is found only under the eyelids of hippopotami, living on the beasts' tears.

Flying biters are not easily confused with fleas. What tends to baffle more is the difference between fleas and human lice, bedbugs, ticks, mites, harvest-mites—the wingless brood. Ticks and mites belong to the order Acarina. Like spiders they are not insects (having eight instead of six legs), though often thought to be. Humans troubled by them have generally picked them up in fields. Ticks are the larger kind, and the commonest of these are sheep ticks. They lie in wait for sheep in fields, cling when they can to animal fur or human clothing, and plunge their heads into the skin for a blood meal. Replete, they drop back to the grass, and can if necessary wait up to four years for the next mobile canteen. Mites somewhat resemble ticks, but are smaller, many of them microscopic. One causes blackheads on human skin. Another, the scabies mite, brings about violent inflammation. The harvest-mite, the larval stage of one species of mite, is just visible to the human eye and is most commonly seen—though not with equanimity—as a reddish dot on tender skin after a picnic on chalky ground. By this time its mouthparts are buried under the cuticle and it stays for two or three days, causing an intense itching which does not stop after it has dropped off.

The field narrows to human lice, bedbugs and human fleas. Common to all three is the fact that their home is our home, our bodies the snug scene of part of their life's routine. Lice are of many kinds, and there are three races that feed on men. The head louse spends its life amid hair, the body louse seeks out smoother skin, and the pubic louse (or 'crab') is a more unsavoury specialist. Those who suffer from them some-times develop a quick immunity. Several hundreds can exist on one man, but fairly regular washing and changes to clean clothes make it impossible for the colony to survive. (Pubic lice, though, are more obstinate and need chemical cleansing.) In man, therefore, lice are roughly confined to the unhygienic, those who engage in trench warfare, and a few unlucky in love. Nits are the eggs of lice, fixed by a kind of cement to animal hairs, where the shells remain after the larvae break out.

Bugs is an ambiguous word. In America it refers often to any insect. In Britain it has sometimes almost as wide a meaning, but with more unpleasant connotations. It is often used specifically to refer to the bedbug, least popular of parasites. This, full-grown, is about a fifth of an inch long, thin at times but becoming almost circular after a full feed of blood. It lives in dirty houses, laying its eggs in wall-cracks or furniture, and coming out at night to crawl (it has no wings) to exposed flesh, stab painfully and suck. It is brown, rich reddish brown after a feed. Nothing nice has ever been said about it. The root of the word may be the same as that of bogy, and it has been known as the 'terror by night'. It is recorded that people have tried putting bowls of water under the legs of their beds to prevent its nocturnal attacks. The calculating bug, it is said, crawls slowly across the floor, up the wall, along the ceiling till it is over the bed, then drops with a tiny pat to the precincts of its prey.

It remains to treat, at greater length, of fleas.

I

INDICTMENT

'I don't *rejoice* in insects at all,' Alice explained.

That day when an antique flea, waiting in its badger sett or pig's den for the familiar step of its returning provider, heard instead an unfamiliar footfall, smelt a different smell and saw a curious shadow that it had not seen before; and decided still to take a chance; and sprang intrepid on to the hairy flanks of *Homo neanderthalensis* or some relative of his; and, amidst the patchy down, trod warily, stabbed steadily, and deep imbibed the first flea draught of human blood—that day marked the beginning of a lasting but one-sided match. Fleas took to man, and stayed with him, through a turbulent epoch whose earlier reaches are obscured by the illiteracy of *neander-thalensis*. There was no love on man's part, but he could not throw off his new acquaintance. As soon as he found words, after a million years or so, he used them to sublimate his frustrated anger. When he came to write, after another long lapse, he used up much ink and thought on the generally unseen black monster. But, dumb or articulate, man could never physically rid himself of the pest. It may be a reason why the neglected corpus of flea literature contains so much of man's ingenuity and imagination.

Poets, thinkers, diarists, scientists, travellers—all at times turn their minds to the flea. Explorers more than most, because one of the annoyances of fleas is in having long before settled in places that man reaches for the first time. Greeks, Scythians, Romans, Arabs; Spanish conquistadors in the New World, Portuguese Jesuit missionaries to the alien mysticism of

Cathay, hardy pioneers in Australia and America, emigrant and oppressed Europeans seeking a new home in Africa: they have all come across fleas, and cursed their luck. Herodotus, Marco Polo, Mungo Park, Burton, Livingstone—each have recurring references in their writings. Marco Polo speaks of Indian noblemen raising their beds aloft by means of pulleys attached to the ceiling to escape the nocturnal attacks of fleas. The priests of old Egypt, according to Herodotus, shaved their heads every three days to stay free, at least in that quarter, from the vermin; and E. W. Lane, a modern Herodotus, tells that the flea situation improved little in Egypt over the centuries and that fleas in winter are 'excessively numerous', the locals making it worse by seldom changing their clothes, awake or asleep.

Wherever they go, they all complain. In Rome, Nathaniel Hawthorne finds that fleas 'come home to everybody's business and bosom'. Another suffers among the plains of Turkestan. As they trek across the wilderness of America, early pioneers complete their diaries with a vexed daily tally. 'Our hammocks are infested with fleas'—so wrote J. L. Williams, opening up the torrid swamps of Florida bordering the Gulf of Mexico. Lewis and Clark, sent to survey the new territory of Louisiana, acquired from Napoleon for fifteen million dollars, itch and execrate the whole trip through. And in the late nineteenth century Sanborn reaches the west coast only to find the Indians of California 'repulsive stolid creatures, with sullen stare, long be-vermined locks, and filthy blankets full of fleas'. It is a sad story, but a tribute to the prolific success of the flea in getting itself about.

Wherever the flea got, and man came too, it bothered him, sometimes out of his mind. Man was impotent to destroy it, and impatient to bear it. He turned it into a symbol of all he disliked. It became the perennial succubus, image of all that vexed and irked, and was mean and small and sucked the blood and throve on filth. From a chance meeting in a cave, the flea stole gradually forward to the consciousness of man, and from there to all the diversity that consciousness has created. It was established in myth and saga, romance and poem, art and drama. It had whole operas written about it, and songs in other operas, and Chaliapin became famous singing one of them. It has even had a place in religion, and on occasion been an object of worship itself.

In the main, however, mankind has frowned on the flea. It is an irritant, causing bother and itches down the ages. It is a speck of dirt, insidious dirt, a symbol of all dirty and insidious things. It is diminutive in bodily and moral stature, standing for those things whose small size earns only contempt. Fourth, it is a bloodsucker. Not a Gothic vampire to chill the marrow; but a vexing, dirty, diminutive bloodsucker, stealing our life-blood with a proboscis, not fangs, and leaving as the token of its felony a petty, red and irking pimple. It is bothersome, scabrous, tiny and parasitical, and the testimony is a seam of anger and contempt that runs through the world's literature.

'After whom is the King of Israel come out?' calls David the slayer of Goliath, adding the only mention of the flea in the Bible: 'After whom dost thou pursue? after a dead dog, after a flea?' Implicit in the self-scorn is the assumption that fleas are despicably small, or perhaps less small than petty, less minute than midget. A snowflake, a dewdrop, a tiny jewel appeal to people, and in Japan a cult has evolved of the miniature. But fleas are on the side of ticks, worms, elves, dwarfs and goblins. They are bracketed with small minds, small views, small purses. Fictional fleas have often been made in the like-ness of misers. Few of the many who mentioned it have found anything nicely little about the flea.

From time to time the irritations of fleas have been put to lofty use. This was especially true in the Dark Ages, soon after missions brought the codes of eastern desert hermits to Europe. Ireland quickly took the lead in western asceticism, and the Irish, feeling that man's pain was God's pleasure, devised novel means to prove their sanctity. None more than

Tulchan's son who, while his friends recited psalms neck-high in cold streams, or spent nights naked on nettles or mountain-tops or in occupied coffins, practised a discipline of admirable economy. He never scratched himself. Fleas assured him of a lifetime's torment.

With variants,* the tradition prospered in the Middle Ages, and even later. St Francis of Assisi not only tolerated, he virtually embraced bodily parasites. To him they were 'the pearls of poverty' and riches for their own sake. Cardinal Bellarmine, bastion of the counter-Reformation who was canonised in 1930, displayed his saintly altruism in the matter of fleabites. 'We shall have Heaven to reward us for our suffer-ings,' he said, 'but these poor creatures have nothing but the enjoyment of this present life.' Bellarmine's example passed to his pupil, the good St Aloysius, who renounced title and riches to serve those smitten by plague in Rome. After a time he succumbed himself and died, but lives on in literature as the benign hero of one of the *Ingoldsby Legends*, who

> Though his cassock was swarming
> With all sorts of vermin,
> He'd not take the life of a flea!

It is ironic that fleas, carriers of plague, took his.

There was no getting away from vermin in those days. When Thomas à Becket was murdered in 1170 and prepared for the grave, his robes were found by those who stripped him to 'seethe with lice'. There may have been some intention here of mortifying the body, but at that time even if you were king of England it was necessary to choose between the chill of frequent changing and growing infestation. Matters were no different four hundred years later at the court of Henry VIII. When in 1962 parts of old Whitehall Palace were

---

* St. Evlalia (who filled her bed with sea-urchins each night), regularly caught the many fleas in her blanket, counted them, separated males from females, set them free, and began again. She lived but twelve years.

uncovered during alterations to the Treasury, a wardrobe was exposed for the first time since the sixteenth century. Among the tucks of the clothes inside were many intact, mummified bodies of early Tudor fleas. Clearly blue blood was as succulent as red. Like death, fleas gave no indemnity to kings.

Even if the rich had known how to rid themselves, their servants would have refilled the flea ranks when they made their masters' beds, or mended their clothes or polished their boots. In a sense fleas had to be accepted. The habit of crack⁄ing them in public was deprecated, but it was the execution more than the presence of fleas that gave offence. 'Though they trouble us much', wrote Thomas Moufet (father, accord⁄ing to W. S. Bristowe, of that Miss Muffet whom a spider frightened away) in Queen Elizabeth's reign, 'yet they neither stink as Wall lice doe, nor is it any disgrace to a man to be troubled with them, as it is to be lowsie.'*

As at the top, so it was at lower levels of society. 'Hastow been fleen all night, or artow dronke?' asked Chaucer's Manciple. Shakespeare's peasants often moan at unabating irritation. 'I think this be the most villainous house in all London road for fleas', complains a carrier in *Henry IV*. 'Your chamber⁄lie breeds fleas like a loach', grumbles another. In imagery that makes use of the beast Shakespeare is more pro⁄digal. 'Thou flea, thou nit, thou winter⁄cricket thou', Petruchio upbraids his quaking tailor, summoned to fit Kate with un⁄familiar finery. Mistress Ford, with no reflection on Falstaff's size but much on his moral stature, talks of his dying 'a flea's death'. And thus Sir Toby Belch on his blond and weedy friend: 'If he were opened, and you find so much blood in his liver as will clog the foot of a flea, I'll eat the rest of the anatomy'.

No flea image has had greater currency over the ages than that which originated about this time with Rabelais and

---

* There were limits. An attendant of Louis XI one day picked a flea from the King's robe, and was rewarded. Next day a courtier, hoping for similar gain, picked off another. The King had him whipped.

spread fast to all languages. 'This flea', cried Panurge omin-
ously, 'that I have in my ear has been tickling me.' (Panurge
was a great one for fleas. He 'had a great many little hornes
full of fleas and lice which he borrowed from the beggars of

"He went away with a Flea in his Ear."—*Old Saying.*

SKETCH OF A MOST REMARKABLE FLEA WHICH WAS FOUND
IN GENERAL HAYNAU'S EAR.

Cartoon from *Punch* marking the visit to England of General
Haynau, after his tyrannical suppression of the Hungarian
revolution of 1848

St Innocent, and cast them with small canes or quills to write with, into the necks of the daintiest Gentlewomen that he could finde, yea even in the church'.) From his day people were forever being sent away with a flea in the ear. A flea had become a stinging rebuff.

> Then mimick'd my voice with satirical sneer,
> And sent me away with a flea in my ear

a character complains in *Love's Cure* by Beaumont and Fletcher. The phrase constantly recurs. *Punch* used it forcefully to illustrate the vicious reception in England of General Haynau, sadistic suppressor of the Hungarian Revolution of 1848. 'A sketch', ran the caption, 'of a most remarkable flea which was found in General Haynau's ear.' More recently the phrase has been used as the title of a French farce by Georges Feydeau.

After Shakespeare and Rabelais the flea, running the gauntlet of centuries, became victim to the Metaphysicals. Where fleas sucked blood, that sinuous cleric John Donne sucked meaning from the minutest objects and distilled it to universality. Fleas seemed made for his purposes. With him they branch, not for the first time but most elegantly, into erotic literature, becoming a kind of sanctum of physical love. But Donne does not overlook their irritant powers. 'The Flea,' he accuses, with a sly, seventeenth-century dwelling on the diphthong, 'the Flea, though hee kill none, hee does all the harme hee can.'

Elsewhere, through furtive association, Donne found the insect to be rather like women. It might have been in the face of some doxy's betrayal that he embarked on this particular strained parallel:

Women are like . . . Fleas sucking our very blood, who leave not our most retired places free from their familiarity, yet for all their fellowship will they never be tamed or commanded by us.

Fleas of course do suck our blood—it is their bread and water —yet they are simply obeying the dictates of their natures. The same may perhaps be said of Donne's lady, though still the accusation seems forced. Yet a contemporary of Donne went further. George Gascoigne, prototype of the English renais⁄ sance, adept alike with pen and sword, once indulged a morbid mood in which he compared the accoutrements of life with those of death—bed to grave, clothes to mould, and

> The hungry fleas which frisk so fresh
> To worms I can compare,
> Which greedily shall gnaw my flesh
> And leave the bones full bare.

A little dizzy from all these mental contortions, the flea passed on to the eighteenth century, during which it main⁄ tained its needling assault on rationalists who preferred cut and thrust to be cerebral. It might have expected a rational response from Augustan men of letters but this was not to be. Pope, who for want of paper in an impoverished boyhood wrote on any available scraps, developing thus a tiny script and a taste for the minute, knew well of fleas and turned them in his poetry to vicious purposes. Other poets lost all scruple in their attacks, like the unnamed rhymester whose verbal re⁄ venge against the 'Coward Aethiop Vermine' covered several octavo pages:

> Oh how they sting my flesh! was black⁄brow'd night
> And the whist stilnesse of it, made by Fate
> To make man happy or unfortunate?
> If there be any happiness or zest
> In pangs of torture, I am fully blest. . . .
> Their number frights me, not their strength; I'd dare
> The Lion, Panther, Tigar, or the Beare
> To an encounter, to be freed from these
> Relentlesse demy⁄devills, cursed Fleas.

The growing race of pamphleteers, broadsheet-writers, gossips and scandal-mongers, grown bolder after young Pitt brought down the curtain on monarchical rule, took fleas, in a sense, as their allies. Peter Pindar bore for a while the standard of this troupe. He picked any cause, any man or woman for a stream of invective that loses effect by being broad and none too deep. Fleas appear often:

> Ye hopping natives of a hard, hard bed

he writes in his *Elegy to the Fleas of Teneriffe*,

> Whose bones, perchaunce, may ache as well as ours,
> O let us rest in peace the weary head
> This night—the first we ventured to your bowers.

Elsewhere he puts the flea to novel literary use in a diatribe against Sir Joseph Banks, President of the Royal Society and founder of the Royal Botanical Gardens at Kew, who had accompanied Cook on his journey round the world. Banks's house in Soho Square attracted a crowd of sycophants anxious to impress him with new but trivial discoveries. Pindar, hired by Royal Society members frustrated by their President's notorious neglect of their work, pictures a certain Jonas Dryander deferentially entering the room where Banks and his cronies are assembled. Dryander carries a tray of fleas:

> 'I've just boiled fifteen hundred,' Jonas whin'd,
> 'The dev'l a one change colour could I find.'
> Then Jonas curs'd, with many a wicked wish,
> And show'd the stubborn fleas upon a dish.
> 'How!' roar'd the President, and backward fell:
> 'There goes, then, my hypothesis to hell!'

What frontier, ask the alarmed bystanders, has the great man failed to breach? The answer, Sir Joseph being for the while

speechless, is a long time in the coming. At last he tells. From
the resemblance in shape—which is uncanny—he had deduced
that fleas might be stunted lobsters, and a new source of food.
Experiment revealed the awful truth, that 'Fleas are not lobsters,
damn their souls'.

Scientists had before this begun to discover a fascination, a
microcosmic miracle, in the formation of the flea. But to the
layman it remained a tiny torment with no redeeming feature.
There was much eighteenth-century scoffing at those who
tried to examine or dissect the flea, and the scorn gave place
to a recurrent conceit. Pope lampooned those who made
'cages for gnats and chains to yoke a flea'. William Cowper,
in *Charity*, derided those who scrutinised the minute:

> Whether he measure earth, compute the sea,
> Weigh sunbeams, carve a fly, or split a flea;
> The solemn trifler with his boasted skill
> Toils much, and is a solemn trifler still.

The idea passed to proverb. To be mean, hair-splitting,
miserly was 'to flay a flea for hide and tallow'. An American
wit wrote of 'the old school gentleman who split a knife that
cost fourpence, in skinning a flea for his hide and tallow'.
From then on the phrase was in general currency. Scott used
it in *The Abbot*, and others took it from him. The merciless
message was clear: that fleas were contemptible, and should
be beneath our regard.

Dr Johnson, who sided often with the underdog, might
have been more considerate towards fleas. In his house off
Fleet Street he supported a stray Negro, two reformed prosti-
tutes, and a whole community of life's flotsam. Yet without
hesitation he condemned fleas, when asked which of two
minor poets he considered the better. 'Sir,' he replied, 'there is
no settling the point of precedency between a louse and a flea.'
A few years later Robert Southey, more pleased than the
critics with his own epic *Joan of Arc*, wrote to a friend: 'The

newspapers are at me; I am used to flea-bites, and never scratch a pimple to a sore.' Later in the century Disraeli could laugh off the National Debt as a fleabite.

A nonentity. Something it is vain to strive after, beneath consideration; any concern with which exposes the vanity of human wishes. The vain man, Erasmus had said, 'invokes heaven if a flea bites him'. La Fontaine had written a fable with the same gist:

> A fool had his shoulder bitten by a flea, which lodged in a fold of his coat. 'Hercules,' cried the man, 'you should rid the earth of this monster that visits us each spring. Jupiter on high, what stops you? Why won't you destroy the race and avenge me?' To kill a flea he would have forced heaven to lend him thunderbolt and bludgeon.

'It seems', La Fontaine moralised, 'that the most insignificant men, at every step and trifle, must vex Olympus and everyone there as if the Trojan War were on again.' For which the Spanish, though well endowed with moles and mountains, have an aphorism of their own. *Hacer de una pulga un elefante*, they say—to turn a flea into an elephant.

Understandably the age of Victoria left most things about fleas unsaid. Horror was such that the subject was suppressed, like sex and other backslidings. Fleas appear, of course, in the documents of social distress and again in the abundant erotica of Victorian gentlemen who entertained more urges than those to serve Queen and Country. As far as possible, however, fleas and all reference to them were outcast from society. This may have had something to do with the most extraordinary appearance of a flea in literature, which had occurred a few years before Victoria's accession. The episode fits as oddly into the social history of fleas as its creator into the broad development of the English literary tradition.

William Blake's best-known songs for children were a far cry from his tangled flea vision. They were the playful reflections from a furnace, the whimsy of Hamlet. His flea was dark and foreboding, a symbol of unalloyed evil. It was a flea from hell.

In his early sixties, Blake had met John Varley, an artist, a teacher of art and a charmer with a confused but fanatical interest in astrology, physiognomy and related pursuits. Both explored the twilight of men's minds, but one was a prophet and the other a bit of a quack. Surface links, however, brought them often together and Varley, in their long lucu-brations, was able to persuade Blake that he, Blake, was in touch with other-worldly spirits. One cannot for sure say he was not.

Among many others, it seems that Moses, David, Caesar, Solomon, Socrates, the Lionheart and Milton's first wife came before Blake, to say their say and sometimes pose for a portrait. Saul, King of Israel, had to return, since one sitting was too short for an accurate likeness. A few of the subjects were play-ful, others doleful or bitter. Hotspur confided that he was 'indignant to be killed by such a person as Prince Henry, who was so much his inferior'.

The extant collection of these portraits is known as the Visionary Heads, and the one Varley called 'the greatest curiosity of all' was the ghost of a flea. It appeared one night between the hours of midnight and two as both men sat in profound anticipation by the fire in Varley's study. Feeling the flea's appearance impending, Blake asked his friend for pencil and paper. 'I see him now before me', said Blake, and sketched a likeness. 'I felt convinced', Varley wrote later, 'by his mode of proceeding, that he had a real image before him, for he left off, and began on another part of the paper, to make a separate drawing of the mouth of the Flea, which the spirit having opened, he was prevented from proceeding with the first sketch till he had closed it.' Both sketches recently turned up in a Scottish collection.

Varley was able to use the pictures, and the information the flea gave, in his bosky *Treatise on Zodiacal Physiognomy*. This contained, among other sensations, 'new and astrological explanations of some remarkable portions of ancient mytho-logy'. With the aid of the sketches he was able to class fleas squarely under the sign of Gemini, for the flea's 'brown colour is appropriate to the colour of the eyes in some full-toned Gemini persons. And the neatness, elasticity, and tense-ness of the Flea, are significant of the elegant dancing and fencing sign Gemini.'

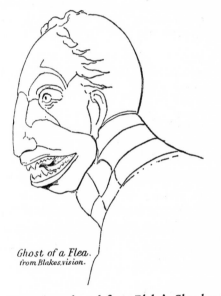

Ghost of a Flea.
from Blakes vision.

Engraving adapted from Blake's Sketches by
John Varley for his *Treatise on Zodiacal
Physiognomy*, 1828

The visitor's disclosures about the true nature of its kind were more interesting. They were an awesome revelation, much to the taste of those who see no good in the insect. For as the rebels among angels were cast down with Lucifer, so the most destructive of men—this flea would have us believe—are consigned to fleas' frames to keep them from overmuch mischief. All fleas, it confided to Blake, were 'inhabited by the souls of such men as were by nature bloodthirsty to excess, and were therefore providentially confined to the size and form of insects; otherwise, were he himself for instance the size and form of a horse, he would depopulate a great portion of the country'. In curious conclusion he added that 'if in attempting to leap from one island to another, he should fall into the sea, he could swim, and should not be lost'.

Blake's flea is in the shape of a thick-set and muscle-bound man. His back is arched. Two long pigtails hang from his stubbly head. Behind him large stars shine, framed by thick curtains. His fingers extend to claws and in one hand he holds a bowl, evidently for blood. His tongue is long, sharp and upward coiled. He closely resembles images of the devil.

At no other point did the flea achieve such invidious proportions. There are related references. A boy in *Henry V* talks with Mistress Quickly's companions about the dead Falstaff. 'Do you not remember', he says, 'a' saw a flea stick upon Bardolph's nose, and a' said it was a black soul burning in hell fire.' To this day gypsies of Bohemia know fleas as 'Satan's horses'. But only Blake was granted a full confession.

†   †   †

The attitude of the Victorian gentleman towards domestic fleas was thoroughly squeamish. Beyond Europe's borders he could be sick with malaria or quartan fever, could brave wild beasts, dirt, disease, rancid food, no food at all, even the prospect of becoming food at a cannibal feast—in order to trace the Nile's source or bring the gospel to Pygmies and Hottentots. But at home things must be right; he became fanatical in pursuing those twin aims of godliness and cleanliness. His dearest wish, where fleas were concerned, was to exterminate

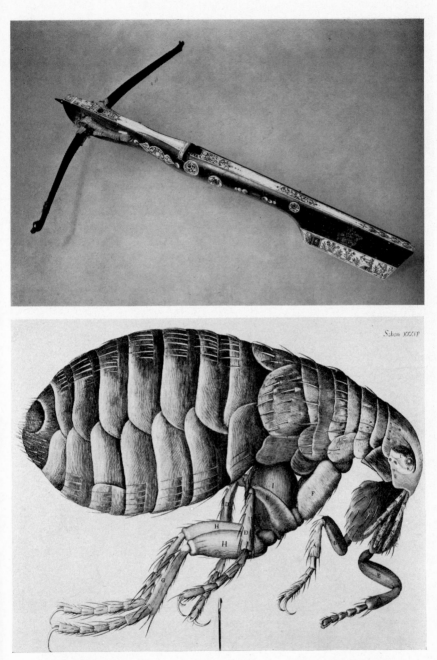

Seventeenth-century miniature cannon in the Arsenal, Stockholm, supposedly used by Queen Christina to shoot at fleas, according to Linnaeus and others

One of the earliest detailed engravings of a flea, from Robert Hooke's *Micrographia*, 1665

The Ghost of a Flea, by William Blake, painted from sketches supposedly made in the ghost's presence

them. He seldom mentioned them. Remembering an inn in Milan where he passed a sleepless night, Trollope could exclaim: 'Ah, there were so many in those beds!' but could not give a name to his tormentors.

But not all Victorians were gentlemen, and some who were sometimes broke the taboo. One of these was the younger Thomas Hood, who chose to take off Edgar Allen Poe's *Annabel Lee* in a short parody called *The Cannibal Flea*.

> It was many and many a year ago,
>   In a District styled E.C.,
> That a monster dwelt whom I came to know
>   By the name of Cannibal Flea,
> And the brute was possessed of no other thought
>   Than to live—and live on me.

Even so, the horror of fleas was mildly expressed. It was left to lower social orders, who suffered worse, to express it better. In sailors' slang an unsavoury bed became a flea-bag, a rotten hovel flea-pit. The word 'pants' was extended by those unused to these garments being clean to 'fleas and ants'; so too a 'house', euphemistic for brothel, was split and rhymed to emerge as 'flea and louse'. A time came when the men who made use of them began to speak of 'catching fleas with' Sue or Molly— a coarse paraphrase, but with delicate points. One witty enemy of the English north country devised new arms for the county of York, comprising a fly, a flea and a flitch of bacon. The fly, it was said, drinks of anyone's cup. The flea will suck anyone's blood. While bacon is no good until it is hung.

The present century, released from old taboos, has less cause for preoccupation with fleas. Even so, while armed with powders and fumigants, detractors remain. 'Was there ever dog that praised his fleas?' Yeats wrote to a poet 'who would have me praise certain Bad Poets and Imitators.' Yeats often made reference, never kindly, to fleas. His characters are always rummaging for them, sometimes with the good fortune of one of the Three Hermits who 'caught and cracked his flea'. Belloc wrote of the 'fleas that tease in the high Pyrenees', and the great mass of other mentions in twentieth-century literature bespeaks the insect's continuing menace. As in Donne's time, he does 'all the harme hee can'.

Yet, for the people of the West, this harm is less than before. Science, in Britain and America, has put human fleas on the run, and many modern allusions are to conditions elsewhere. Two classic accounts, both from the same pen, best illustrate the trend. In the first, self-exiled Norman Douglas recalls 'a long-drawn golden evening among the Cyclades', when 'the movement of Nature seemed to be momentarily arrested'. He sailed past an imposing island, and 'here if anywhere, me-thought, Sirens might still dwell unmolested'. But while he climbed ashore his knowing boatman remained on board. In an instant, Douglas was disenchanted:

> It was no Siren islet. It was an islet of fleas. I picked them off my clothes in tens, in hundreds, in handfuls. Never was mortal nearer jumping out of his skin. . . .
>
> Now whether these fleas had inhabited the island from time immemorial, being degenerate descendants of certain heroic creatures that sailed thither in company of Jason and his Argonauts, or had been left there by shipwrecked mariners of modern days; how it came about that they multiplied to the exclusion of every other living thing; what manner of food was theirs—whether, anthropophagous-wise, they preyed upon one another or had learned to content themselves with the silvery dews of morning, like Anacreon's cicada, or else had acquired the faculty of long fasting be-tween orgies such as they enjoyed on that afternoon; these and other questions have since occurred to me as not unworthy of consideration. . . . At that moment I was far too busy to give any thought to such matters.

Some years later, travelling in Old Calabria in search of local myth and *mores,* Douglas put up at an inn, an exceedingly humble inn:

> It was not long ere I discovered there was another bed in this den, opposite my own; and, judging by certain undulatory and saltatory movements within, was occupied. Presently the head of a youth emerged, with closed eyes and flushed features. He indulged in a series of groans and spasmodic kicks, that subsided once more, only to recommence. . . .
>
> 'This poor young man' I thought 'is plainly in bad case. On account of illness he has been left behind by the rest of the band. He is feverish, or possibly subject to fits, to choriasis or who knows what disorder of the nervous system. A cruel trick to leave a suffering youngster alone in this foul hovel.' I misliked his symptoms—that anguished complexion and delirious intermittent trembling, and began to run over the scanty stock of household remedies contained in my bag, wondering which of them might apply to his complaint. There was court plaster, and boot polish, quinine, corrosive sublimate, and Worcester sauce (detest‐able stuff but indispensable hereabouts). Just as I had decided in favour of the last‐named, he gave a more than unusually vigorous jerk, sat up in bed, and, opening his eyes, remarked:
>
> 'Those fleas!'

Literature, then, proves it; the sleep‐depriving, bump‐erecting, feathery‐tickling, night‐and‐day‐itching, lunacy‐inducing powers of the pestilential, omnipresent flea. If needed, the wisdom of peasants and tales of old wives reinforce the message. 'Do nothing hastily but catching of fleas', warns a wary proverb; and another—'Sue a flea and catch a bite'. The irking depredations of this midget bloodsucker are everywhere attested. To be dirtier than fleas, it appears, is unimaginable;

and it was with this in mind that Ernie Pyle, American commentator of the Second World War, wrote, 'If you go long enough without a bath even the fleas will let you alone'. From the evidence of all the ages, it seems there is nothing right about a flea.

2

THE VAIN VERDICT

ox: Men are very kind to me. Now and then they pat me on
the head.
FLEA: They'd pat me too if I let them, but I take good care
they don't.

AESOP

In view of all the censure, it was not surprising that man should
try to devise deterrents. He indicted the flea and found it
guilty. Death or exile was the sentence. It was not the verdict
of a day or a month, for whenever man was in touch with fleas
he straightway reached the same conclusion. His troubles
came in executing it, for the flea was usually condemned *in
absentia*. All the same, man was not short of invention.

A Greek treatise on agriculture, the *Geoponica*, included an
informative diatribe against fleas and among other things
advised persons in an infested area to cry 'Ouch! Ouch!' No
flea would touch them after that. It gave a deal more advice
on getting rid of the pest; a compound of exotic concoctions,
sorcerers' recipes, and a little good sense. Part of the list might
have been drawn up by Puck—rhododaphne and absinthium,
roots of the wild cucumber, a decoction of the conyza's root,
quicklime and amurca, with strong brine and sea-water
sprinkled. Lines are to be drawn round dishes in the floor,
cut with swords that had done men to death, then bay-leaves
pounded, or bull's fat smeared, or goat's blood poured. Unfortunately the passage of time has disqualified the rigmaroles.
Only goat's blood would do real good, attracting the fleas and
making them stick.

An old Egyptian remedy, anomalous in the welfare state,

might have worked better. It was to smear a slave with asses' milk and keep him standing awhile in the room. Fleas had eyes (and mouthparts) for none but him. The same method was used for unemployed menials in Arabic countries, and it was customary to send a man into every room of a disused house, to waken all the fleas by his tread and magnetise them by his warmth. After a discreet interval, others would follow, and so save their skins. In the southern states of America sheep have been used for the same purpose.

The Romans were a calculating folk, and it is fitting that the medical writer Cornelius Celsus, in the first century A.D., should have mapped out a somewhat technical procedure for removing fleas from ears. In the first place, 'a little wool is introduced in which it becomes engaged and so is extracted'. This, he acknowledges, may fail. So too may induced sneezing and ear syringes. There remains an extreme and serious course:

> Again, a plank may be arranged, having its middle supported and the ends unsupported. Upon this the patient is tied down with the affected ear downwards, so that the ear projects beyond the end of the plank. Then the end of the plank at the patient's feet is struck with a mallet, and the ear being so jarred what is within drops out.

The elder Pliny, a little later, gave equally detailed advice for avoiding the pest altogether. It was repeated as late as the seventeenth century by the author of *A Thousand Notable Things*: 'If you mark where your right foot doth stand at the first time that you do hear the cuckow, and then grave or take up the earth under the same; wheresoever the same is sprinkled about, there will no fleas breed. I know it hath proved true.'

The character who has come down to us from his fourteenth-century writings as the Goodman of Paris, gave unequivocal instructions to his young wife on the subject (the instructions fill a book and cover every topic of domestic management so minutely that one may doubt if the match was a long one). 'In summer', he commands (in Eileen Power's translation),

> take heed that there be no fleas in your chamber, nor in your bed, the which you may do in six ways, as I have heard tell. . . . But the best way is to guard oneself against those that be within the coverlets and the furs, and the stuff of the dresses wherewith one is covered. For know that I have tried this, and when the coverlets, furs or dresses, wherein there be fleas, be folded and shut tightly up, as in a chest tightly corded with straps, or in a bag well tied up and pressed, or otherwise put and pressed so that the aforesaid fleas be without light and air and kept imprisoned, then will they perish forthwith and die.

'Most bountiful Nature', Moufet notes two hundred years later, 'hath supplied us with a large field of remedies' and he begins a long list with Dwarf Elder leaves, Fern root, or Anchusa, flowers of Pennyroyal, Rue, Coloquintida. 'Above all', he concludes, 'the dregs of Marespisse, or seawater are commended, if they be sprinkled up and down.' In other accounts alder leaves get frequent mentions—a sure preventative if strewn about room or house. While beeswaxing wooden floors hindered fleas from propagating in the cracks.

Country lore contributed advice on *when* to catch fleas. 'If you kill one flea in March you will kill a hundred' runs a proverb; and from all the sources of folklore statements stream in to support the view that in March fleas emerge from their winter quarters to resume the scourging of man. Sometimes the date is specified—March 1st or Easter, assuming that flea feasts are as movable as Christian. Air the beds before Easter, goes one injunction. Close the windows and sweep the doorstep on March 1st, says another, and you will have no fleas all the year.* Dr Johnson's dictionary quotes serious advice from Thomas Tusser, the Elizabethan agriculturist:

> While wormwood hath seed, get a handfull or twaine,
> To save against March, to make flea to refraine.
> Where chamber is sweeped, and wormwood is strown,
> No flea for his life dare abide to be known.

Another rustic contention is that fleas are more active during the rain. 'Fleas thirst for blood, a sign of rain', goes the saying, and is elsewhere substantiated:

> When eager bites the thirsty flea,
> Rain and clouds you sure shall see.

Increased biting forecasts sharper weather:

> When fleas do very many grow,
> Then t'will surely rain or snow.

True it is that fleas have a liking for moisture. Heavier air, presaging rain, makes them, as Moufet—that tireless Herodotus of English natural history—puts it, 'bold to run over every part of man's body'.

So familiar was the blight of fleas among the highest in the land that ladies took to wearing the most decorative appliances to trap them on their bodies. Traps became articles of fashion, like furbelows and exotic beads. A German print shows one kind. It is attached round the neck of a lady whose bosom is bare. From the ribbon a stick hangs between her breasts, a sticky stick within a perforated tube. Fleas, seeking shade, entered the tube's holes and were caught. Another kind was a simple strip of fur. Whether the modern boa has developed from this flea-trap is unknown to me. But the fur was cer-

---

* In this case the details are disputed, creating, one feels, disastrous confusion. A Sussex rhyme instructs:

> If from fleas you would be free
> On the first of March let all your windows *open* be.

tainly worn round the shoulders, and being thicker and darker than any human hair it attracted, and so imprisoned, the fleas. It is also claimed that lap-dogs were selectively bred as living flea-traps, but there can be no proof. To alleviate the effect of bites, women kept long ivory sticks to push amid their elabor- ate coiffures and scratch their scalps.

The Irish peasantry commonly used spearmint and fox- glove plants, American Negroes chinaberry leaves. Mercurial ointment, brimstone, fumigations of some leaves and pot- pourris of others, tied in bags and laid in beds—all have been claimed fatal to the pest. Early American settlers (presumably carrying on European ways) declared that splinters from trees struck by lightning were an effective repellant. In tropical climates, and still often in Africa, cow-dung spread over the floor and hardened (and often patterned with favourite motifs) is said to keep fleas away.

A dubious story describes the remedy of a sham physician marketing his flea-killing powder in Spain. 'Catch the flea,' his instructions ran, 'open its mouth, and place the powder inside. If this course is followed death is guaranteed.'

Hungarian shepherds were once observed to 'grease their linen with hog's lard, and thus render themselves disgusting even to fleas'. In Greece, according to Frazer, fires were kindled on St John's Eve (June 23rd) and the local youths proceeded to jump over them. In this way there was a general purgation, not only of fleas, but of sins too. He also reported that the young men of Sus, in North Africa, similarly leap over glowing embers, chanting, 'We shake on you, O Lady Ashur, fleas and lice and the illnesses of the heart, as also those of the bones'. It was Marco Polo who reported that noblemen in India, whose beds were light cane hammocks swung from the roof, hoisted themselves up at night to put a distance between them and the world-wide prickler.

None of these compare with the stealthy calculation of the fox, whose sly remedy has been seen and reported by many.

The fox tugs up a chunk of moss by the riverside and keeps it protruding from his mouth. He steps backward into the shallows of the river and proceeds slowly, while water laps his legs, his lower body, his pendant tail, his back, his neck. At last his nose alone remains above water. By now it is a densely populated nose, for his fleas, disturbed by the rising flood, have kept climbing till they are marooned on the snout. The last stage begins. The nose itself descends and the beast holds his breath. The fleas walk or spring to the moss, their final refuge. When the last flea is safely transplanted the wily animal opens his mouth, or as some have it, utters a satisfied 'Ah'. The moss and fleas float downstream. 'And so', says Moufet, 'very froliquely being delivered from their molestation', the fox swims back to land.

3

IN FAVOUR OF FLEAS

They say a reasonable amount o' fleas is good for a dog—
keeps him from broodin' over bein' a dog, mebbe.

EDWARD NOYES WESTCOTT

The odd thing is that somewhere in man's inscrutable bosom
there does lurk a soft spot for the flea. Some curious wayward-
ness, not found in its sucking cousins—lice, ticks, mites, mosquitoes, bedbugs—somewhat redeems its record. Some people
even like it. There comes at last a tide in the affairs of fleas.

Even before the days of microscopes Marlowe could write
appreciatively of 'a little pretty frisking flea'. Later, and
especially among biologists, the appreciation grew. Karl
Jordan, one of the greatest of fleaologists, called them the
jolliest of creatures; and he had reason for knowing, for up to
his nineties he would often remain till midnight at his microscope at Tring, examining the different species. That non-
conformist poet W. H. Davies, extolling the free life of tramps,
found other reasons to be fond of them:

> Poor lords and ladies, what tame sport
> To hunt a fox or stag, while we
> Sit on a green bank in the sun
> And chase for hours a faster flea;
> Which blesses us from day to day
> With all our faculties in play.

Those who spend a lifetime studying the creature—which a
French poet has called 'a speck of tobacco with a spring in it'
—grow to distinguish species at a glance, and are fonder of
some than others. This is specialist aesthetics, and hinges on
the differences between combs, antennae and the like; but I

have heard picturesque language used by those to whom the distinctions are automatic.

A. P. Herbert attributed the normally hostile attitude of humans to jealousy:

> I never know why it should be
> So rude to talk about the flea.
> What funny folk we are.
> I think we've got the jealous hump
> Because we know we'll never jump
> So skilfully and far.

Jealousy certainly focussed on a flea well known to music-lovers. This particular flea was patronised by a German king. It was treated as the king's son, decked in a robe of silken velvet, and given chancellor's rank. Everybody had to pay it court, and though

All the lords and ladies, and all the squires and knights,

> There's a wealthy old man of Tabreez
> With a maudlin affection for fleas.
> He'll grin with delight
> When they scratch him and bite—
> Perverted old man of Tabreez!

W. M. Thackeray's *Wealthy Old Man of Tabreez*; one of several drawings-with-limericks sketched by Thackeray and friends of his, perhaps to amuse themselves one evening

The queen and all her maidens, were itching from their
  bites,

nobody could lay a finger upon it, or even be seen scratching.
It lived to a ripe old age, according to Goethe, its creator.
And it lives still in the opera composed by Mussorgsky to
the words of Goethe's *Faust*.*

Always implicit in jealousy is a streak of admiration. But
reactions to the flea do not stop at admiration even. It is the
insect's unique achievement to have run the gamut of abuse
and invective and to emerge, here and there, as an object of
veneration. No comment can enhance the original evidence,
though a word of caution on its source may be of value. It
comes, verbatim, from that enthusiastic nineteenth-century
master of the flea circus, Signor L. Bertolotto:

> At Surat, fleas, bugs and other vermin are held in such
> veneration that they have an hospital endowed, where every
> night some poor fellow, for hire, suffers himself to be tied
> down upon a bed and the vermin feast upon his body. In
> Turkey there is a similar foundation for decayed dogs, an
> institution less ridiculous than the other.

And thus Marco Polo, minutely describing the habits of the
abstinent Yogi, an order in the kingdom of Maabar who walk
naked because they feel no shame concerning anything they
thereby expose 'because we commit no sin'.

> I assure you further that they would not kill any creature or
> any living thing in the world, neither fly nor flea nor louse
> nor any other vermin, because they say they have souls.

It is but one specific reference to the popular oriental ideas of
reincarnation. A flea was (and is) as likely to be aunt or
grandfather as the more acceptable cow or camel. It remains

---

* Since Mussorgsky, the flea has had a whole opera to itself. Ghedini's
La pulce d'oro tells of a flea, an insect Midas, that turned all it bit to gold, with
tragic results.

only to add the staunch conviction of the tribe of Aitutaki, a Polynesian race who linked the tyranny of the insects with that of colonial oppression. For them, according to W. W. Gill, fleas were the departed spirits of white men, and to be treated with respect.

For anything, godly or base, to be properly accepted, it is necessary that something about it be funny. It was a major protestant discovery that Christianity had room for humour. And something to laugh about, as most people know, is good for breaking the ice. So, with fleas, first arraigned with an almost inexhaustible list of complaints, then swung on opinion's pendulum to some recherché brands of worship, it is essential, for their complete purgation, to find if they afford a joke or two. They do. Puns. A form which the Anglo-Saxon likes well, even while he crinkles his nose in distaste.

The jokes do not rise very high. They come best with a monotone patter. 'And then did you hear the one about the tramp that asked another tramp on the bench, "What's a parasite, Alf?"—he was reading an old newspaper and had just seen the word—and Alf said to him, shrugging his shoulders, "Search me".' 'And there was the one about a man sitting outside a flea circus with his dog that was scratching and another man asked the first man why he was scratching and he said, "He went in and stole the show".' 'Or the two fleas going on a journey and one said to the other, "Shall we walk or take a dog?"' 'Or the man who went fishing and caught nothing and looked at his dog scratching itself and said, "I'm glad someone here's got a bite".'

Not very high at all. But they come out well enough with a microphone and an audience in good humour.

Newspapers have a peculiar feeling for the funny side of fleas. They tend in fact to regard everything about fleas as funny. In a short capsuled item of bold print they will include the latest discovery of a new species of flea, somewhere in

Manchuria, in the correct but still enigmatic view that the reader's fancy will be tickled. Such items are headed and sub-headed with phrases like the following: 'He's got the bug for it', or 'Federenko starts from scratch' or 'Once-bitten Horace fights shy'. They also often include jokes like the music-hall ones mentioned, and in so doing seldom include a line that has not gone round several previous generations of readers. Often too they put cartoons with their jokes. It might be in this way: the picture shows a large but legless flea observed by two men. 'It's been proved', says one, 'that fleas have their hearing organs in their legs.' 'How come?' rejoins the other. 'Well, cut off their legs, say "Jump," and they don't, because now they can't hear.' Or they put in passers of time like:

> The arithemetic flea
> Adds to your misery
> Subtracts your pleasure
> Divides your attention
> And multiplies like the devil.

Or simple drawings like this

with the caption 'Jumping flea, with hiccups'.

Finally, it would be wrong to omit the use made of the flea in those irregular snatches sung by children in their games, to help stamp on their inner minds the innate metres of language.

> You naughty flea
> You bit my knee

or

> O dear me
> mother caught a flea
> put it in the teapot
> and made a cup of tea

in which the following sometimes stands for the last two lines:

> flea died, mother cried;
> out goes she.

Fleas also appear in tongue-twisters:

> A flea and a fly flew up in a flue.
> Said the flea to the fly, 'Oh what shall we do?'
> 'Let us flee,' said the fly;
> 'Let us fly,' said the flea;
> So they fluttered and flew up a flaw in the flue.*

In ways like this, in the games and the wisecracks and cartoons and sometimes stoic humour, the flea, against enormous odds, has crept not only into our beds and clothes but into an assured corner of our affections. In this light, the list of its accusers assumes the appearance of suppression.

† † †

It was Socrates' boast, taunting the court that tried him, that all his life he had been the gad-fly of the Athenian people, a goad pricking their sedentary flanks. In clear reverse, fleas might claim to have been the Socrates of the human race. They have ever been pointing morals at us, chastening complacence, deflating conceit. They have pricked our vanity besides our epidermises. They can, in sum, bring us down a peg or two.

Again, I anthropomorphise. It is men who moralise, men who compress the segments of their mental rear legs and bound to the skies of imagination. A flea's leap is a measured eight inches high, and for all anyone knows the flea has no imagination at all. Men attribute to it thoughts and motives quite untranslatable into the terms of its miniature world. Still,

* Several different versions exist.

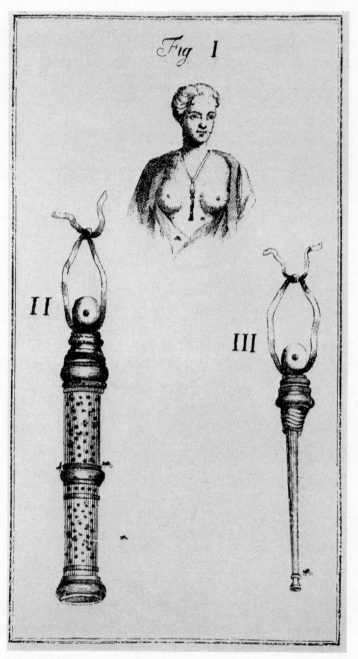

An old decorative flea-trap for women to wear. Cooperative fleas entered the outer perforations and were caught on a sticky tube inside

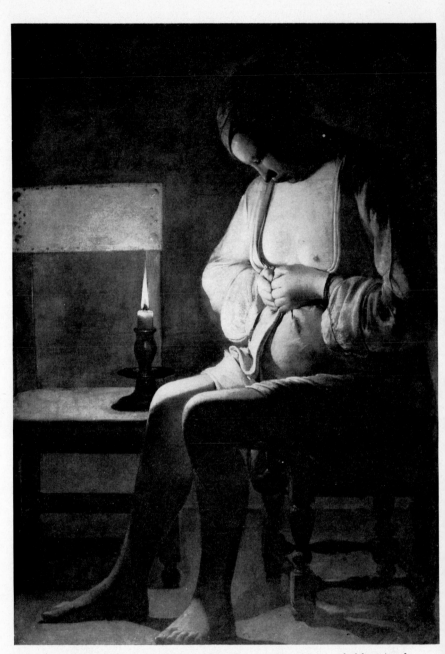

The Flea by Georges de la Tour, early seventeenth century, probably painted more from an interest in chiaroscuro than fleas; now in the Musée Historique Lorrain, Nancy

somehow the flea helps man see himself—points a by-way that leads closest to the truth.

Greeks, Romans and Celts found gods for their purposes— gods with shapes and minds of men but more power to exploit them, to show their use or dangers, to point morals. All the heroes and demigods and nymphs and satyrs and nereids were models of aspects of man, and helped him see himself. After the divine and immortal, animals were used to sharpen focus. Aesop, Christ, La Fontaine, Lewis Carroll and a hundred poets used them. Some chose elves, fairies and goblins. Swift took equine Houynhnms and the little men of Lilliput, Plato and Bunyan abstract virtues and vices, Mary Shelley monsters, Freud the ego, id and super-ego. Some chose fleas.

In all this process of moralising, of personalising anything but man to show the merits and defects of man, the flea has played an inconsistent role. He has been sometimes good, sometimes bad, now showing man's folly, now his virtue. Above all, he has served to prick man's vanity, to show the towering nonsense of his ambition. 'Man,' Montaigne wrote, 'is certainly stark mad; he cannot make a flea, and yet he will be making gods by dozens.' 'You may as well say', says Orleans in *Henry V*, decrying the foolhardiness of the English, 'that's a valiant flea that dare eat his breakfast on the lip of a lion.'

The fact remains, it *is* men who created correcting fleas. Men, who for effect have put the words of castigation into fleas, adding a dimension of experience by the contrived inclusion of another species. One of them was John Gay, author of *The Beggar's Opera* and a genius mercifully resistant to the sensitive, unsmiling guardians of the Hanoverian court, who most wittily stated the theme. The poem, *The Man and the Flea*, is too long to quote in full. It deals with what might be called group solipsism, or collective egoism, showing each of an ascending order of living creatures stating a belief in its own ultimate and unrivalled importance. The snail begins, the crab follows, and he in turn yields to the hawk. The conceit of each is pricked by him who follows, whose nutri∕tional purposes he serves. At length comes man himself, almost top of the ladder of vanity:

> His contemplation thus began:
> When I behold this glorious show,
> And the wide wat'ry world below,
> The scaly people of the main,
> The beasts that range the wood or plain,
> The wing'd inhabitants of air,
> The day, the night, the various year,
> And know all these by Heav'n design'd
> As gifts to pleasure human kind,
> I cannot raise my worth too high;
> Of what vast consequence am I!

to which a small voice gives direct answer:

> Not of th' importance you suppose,
> (Replies a Flea upon his nose;)
> Be humble, learn thyself to scan:
> Know, pride was never made for man.
> 'Tis vanity that swells thy mind.
> What, heav'n and earth for thee design'd!
> For thee, made only for our need,
> That more important Fleas may feed.

Aesop made much of fleas for moral purposes. There are few workaday objects of which he did not make use, but the flea has more than a fair share of appearances. There are fables of fleas and various men, and the lessons learned from the encounter by the men; of a flea and an ox, a flea and a camel, and many others. Two have particular charm, enhanced by the syntax and spelling in the sixteenth∕century translation by Caxton's successor, Richard Pinson.

He that doth evyl, how be it that ye euvyl be nat great, men ought nat to leve hym unpunysshed, as it apereth by thys fable of a man which toke a flee. Yt bote hym, to whom the man sayde in thys maner, Fle why bitest thou me & latest me nat slepe. And the fle answerd it is my kynde to do so, wherfore I pray the yt thou wylt nat putt me to deth. And the man began to laughe and saide to the fle thou maiste me nat hurt sore, neverthelesse the behoveth nat to byte me. wherfore thou shalt dye. For men ought nat to leve no evill unpunysshed, howe be it that it be nat greate.

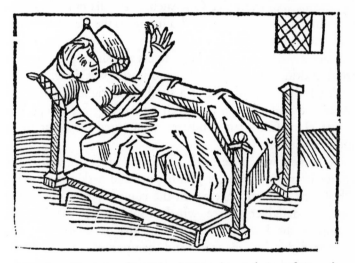

Woodcut illustration for Richard Pinson's translation of Aesop's
The Man and the Flea, 1500

The second tale, of the flea and the camel, shows the insect in no better light, but with a brighter fate. 'He that hathe no myghte', it begins sensibly, 'ought nat to gloryfye ne preise hymself of no thinge.' It tells how a heavily burdened camel went on a long journey, during which a flea jumped up to its hind quarters to enjoy the ride. All day the camel plodded. In the evening it reached the stable it had been making for.

Thereupon the flea jumped down and came round to the front of the animal. It had, it explained, taken pity on the camel, and would no more burden it with its weight. With measured courtesy the camel replied that it mattered neither way to him. 'And therefore', Pinson concludes in what is neither wholly a *sequitur* nor strictly grammatical, 'of hym whiche may neyther helpe ne let nede nat make greate estymacyon of.'

In straight fiction, too, fleas have pointed morals, without being specifically created for the purpose. They teach lessons by unconscious example. One such story tells of a vagabond intending to rob the king. A flea living on the man overheard, and resolved to baulk his plans. When the robber crept into the king's bedroom the flea leapt across and sharply stabbed the royal midriff. The king awoke, and justice was done.

An Indian legend tells of a similarly upright flea that re-stored a dumb princess to speech by entering her throat. But it was Hans Christian Andersen who raised the beast to its most honourable pitch.

A contest was once held, so his tale goes, in which the competitors were a flea, a grasshopper and a skipjack beetle. They were brought together in the company of a great king and his daughter to see which could jump the highest. Naturally the king offered his daughter as prize. The flea impressed by his manners and composure—result of the genteel blood in his veins and his ability to mix with people. The grasshopper had a pedigree going back to Egypt and was contemptuously boastful. The skipjack said nothing, but revealed by the colour of his back whether next winter would be mild or severe. At the appointed hour they began to jump, and the flea sprang first. It was a breath-taking jump, but so high that no-one saw him. It was therefore agreed that he had not jumped at all. The flea was out of the running. Next the grasshopper, who made the mistake of landing upon the king. He was out too. Finally the silent skipjack sprang, after a long contemplative pause. It was a small jump and very unsteady, but it brought him to the lap of the princess, sitting on a low stool. The king was delighted by the gesture. He has legs in his head, he remarked of the skipjack, and granted him his daughter. The grasshopper was affronted, and moped over his defeat. He turned to song, and of course that is how his grating chirp came about. But the chief character to emerge is the flea. Cheerfully accepting an unfair verdict— 'One needs a body to be seen in this world'—he went off to the wars and died in battle. Lithe and courtly, smiling at injustice, he shared the fate of a Byron or a Saint-Exupéry, and like them will always be remembered for it.

4

IMMORAL FLEAS

Man's whole frame is obvious to a flea.

POPE

Amid the plains of French Poitou, still westerly enough to be salted by Atlantic breezes, a complacent feudalism continued long after the storm of the Reformation. There was enlightenment, but of that happy kind which rests on the unbroken structure of what went before. It risked little but the stability of unborn generations. Anything at all could be freely discussed, but all discussion stayed within the bounds of the salon. And each year, during the *Grands-Jours* at Poitiers, there was more talk than usual because many more of the gentry gathered to measure their wits. Women were often the centre of both attraction and discourse. They were the first bluestockings, eloquent descendants of the dumb decorations of the courts of Aquitaine.

Talk was not all of the highest. Often its level was that of Molière's *précieuses* and *demi-mondaines*. Verbiage wrapped in Petrarchan ribbons.

In 1579 the usual pillars of the community gathered at the house of Sieur Desroches and his wife Madeleine. Much was made of the talents, grace and beauty of their daughter Catherine, just come of age and a fair object for the poetic rills of ageing aesthetes. Catherine smiled, simpered and enjoyed the novelty of attention while provincial poets strained provincial minds to catch sensuous beauty in couplets. One afternoon Étienne Pasquier, looking perhaps for the spark of inspiration at Catherine's white aspirant bosom, noticed instead a flea, *'parquée au beau milieu du sein'*. Such temerity, said he 'to "settle" in the very midst of the bosom'. Such enviable luck, said another. Pasquier contrived a verse, with envy its theme. Demoiselle Desroches aired a coy reply. In those moments a literary tradition was born.

All the poets and magistrates and fustian clerics present set out to celebrate the flea. They did so in French, Spanish, Latin, Greek. The matter became a collective serenade, a commotion of pedantic prowess. Pasquier wrote down all he heard, and his collection was last reprinted in France in 1868. It is gruesomely effusive, a tome of monotony pricked with nice conceits. Most of the admirers wondered where

> that proud memorable flea
> mankind one morning stared to see
> on Catherine Desroches' bared breast
> sucking imperturbably

could hop to next, and most of them thought of the same place, describing it with most tortuous rhetoric. They were not the best exploiters of their invention, but they invented nevertheless.

There are those who give the tradition a longer pedigree. 'I am like to Ovid's flea,' says a character in Marlowe's *Faust*; 'I can creep into every corner of a wench.' There are like references in other works. Further, a Latin poem in which a flea profanes a lady's privities has been ascribed to Ovid. For Ovid, to be sure, physical love was a poetic preoccupation. But this composition lacks his lightness of touch. The narrator jibs at the flea for lacerating a tender female body, spotting it with black hillocks, disturbing her sleep, trespassing on 'the parts of lust'. Then he imagines himself a flea insinuating himself into that haven he desired and returning to man's form. Would she call her servants to drive him off? If so, back he'd change into a flea, tormenting her to submission. Success would crown his metamorphoses, however many he was constrained to make.

Ovid, pseudo-Ovid, or more probably Pasquier and his friends, paved the way for the metaphysicals, who reappear here with more satisfying cerebral contortions. They brought the flea theme to their amorous longings and frustrations, and turned out some of their nicer verse. A seventeenth-century Anon took up the Desroches cry directly:

> Madam that flea that crept between your breasts
> I envied, that there he should make his rest:
> The little Creatures fortune was soe good
> That Angells feed not on so pretious foode.
> How it did sucke how eager tickle you
> (Madam shall fleas before me tickle you?)
> Oh I can not holde: pardon if I kild it.
> Sweet Blood, to you I aske this, that which fild it
> Ran from my Ladies Brest. Come happie flea
> That dide for suckinge of that milkie Sea.
> Oh now againe I well could wish thee there,
> About hir Hart, about her anywhere;
> I would vowe (Dearest flea) thou shouldst not dye,
> If thou couldst sucke from hir hir crueltye.

Then came Donne, with Heath Robinson imagery. We have seen him in acid mood compare women to fleas, persistent bloodsuckers without respect for men's privacy or ears for their protests. Now the sight of a flea, or the thought, or a glimpse of the Desroches *recueil*, brought Donne to vary the simple conceit. His poem, *The Flea*, is certainly one of the classics of the flea *corpus*, and deserves quotation in full:

> Marke but this flea, and marke in this,
> How little that which thou deny'st me is;
> It suck'd me first, and now sucks thee,
> And in this flea our two bloods mingled bee;

46

Thou know'st that this cannot be said
A sinne, nor shame, nor losse of maidenhead,
Yet this enjoyes before it wooe,
And pamper'd swells with one blood made of two,
And this, alas, is more than wee would doe.

Oh stay, three lives in one flea spare,
Where wee almost, yea more than maryed are.
This flea is you and I, and this
Our mariage bed, and mariage temple is;
Though parents grudge, and you, w'are met,
And cloyster'd in these living walls of Jet.
Though use make you apt to kill mee,
Let not to that, selfe murder added bee,
And sacrilege, three sinnes in killing three.

Cruell and sodaine, hast thou since
Purpled thy naile, in blood of innocence?
Wherein could this flea guilty bee,
Except in that drop which it suckt from thee?
Yet thou triumph'st, and saist that thou
Find'st not thy selfe, nor mee the weaker now;
'Tis true, then learne how false, feares be;
Just so much honor, when thou yeeld'st to mee,
Will wast, as this flea's death took life from thee.

If schoolboy illusions spatter this curlicued sophistry, still the plane is high. Donne spoke adolescent dreams with monk-ish maturity. The poem, indeed, is the erotic apex of the literary flea. The rest is more blatant, less cloaked. From here on, the immoral flea is plainly pornographic.

Before going down the scurrilous path, some other, quite non-literary erotic associations of the flea are worth notice. It is of course an amorous creature itself. A glance at the clinging couples in any flea culture shows that; nothing will budge them from embrace. But there are other links. Mortal disease and its companion, the frenzy of despair, have often dusted all taboo from human lust. Fleas bring bubonic plague, a historic killer, to man, and induce the phrenetic orgies of numbered days. They are linked too with dirt, and that degraded state that annuls caution and begs for distracting pleasures, however transient. Besides, their motions cause tickles, incite scratches, reminding men of parts usually for-gotten when clothed. Here and elsewhere fleas and lust live side by side. Further, the itch of a fleabite and that of desire have something in common. The brothel traditionally offered both. Fuddled Stephano, in *The Tempest*, sings a song to make the point, about a shrew called Kate who:

> lov'd not the savour of tar nor of pitch;
> Yet a sailor might scratch her where'er she did itch.
> Then to sea, boys, and let her go hang!

That link, however, which firmly set the flea among the pages of pornography, was different from all these. It lay in the flea's power of seeing. 'Man's whole frame is obvious to a flea,' wrote Pope; man, of course, here being generic, and including significantly women. Since it attached itself to man, the flea has been the great arthropodic voyeur, or Peeping Tom—without, we may guess, concomitant ecstasy. And because of its size, its leap, its graft and its want of shame, it has seen a good deal more than any butler. When Actaeon saw Aphrodite naked in the pool, he was turned into a stag, and gorged by hounds at the affronted goddess's order. Unlike Actaeon and subsequent pryers, who nowadays—according to the law reports—risk limb and reputation in their scramble for a vantage point, the flea can feast his eyes without straying an inch from the daily round. It looks with impunity not only on nudity, but on the natural pairing of attracted nudities.

For the first case we have the evidence of many poets, includ-ing the irrepressible Willart de Grécourt, an eighteenth-century French dilettante whose vain attempts ramble through four volumes of his collected works. 'Very often,' he wrote (and very often he wrote much the same thing, for he was loth to let go of an idea):

> 'très souvent, sans crainte,
> Jusques dans le pays d'Amour
> Elle parcourut toute Aminte'*

elle being the flea and Aminte the French and female Tom, Dick or Harry. Others we have seen and many we shall over‑ look have dealt with the same theme. The second theme, however, while amply dealt with in the annals, has had, understandably, less general circulation.

Only in the most adept hands has pornography reached standards that even admit it to the class of literature. Guarded under lock and key, and hedged with secretive paraphernalia, the bulky British Museum collection contains hardly more style than a volume of logarithms. Brilliance is confined to a few long works and a larger number of once‑in‑a‑lifetime gems. Fleas, for their sins and others, appear often in large works but in none that shine.

They follow their patrons from barrack to bordello, from ballroom to four‑poster, from spacious hall to grimy hovel, and they have a peculiar zest for monasteries and nunneries. After one series of earthy exploits they change carriers and witness the sensual hobbies of another age‑group, another class. A hop changes their way of life. Mainly they are spectators, but there are crimes they cannot condone. These they avert with well‑placed stings. Always, this, to preserve innocence against heavy odds.

The dangers of their lives are many and resemble those of the trapeze artist. They clutch at furbelows and swing from hem to bustle. They penetrate to darkness, drawn by the smell of blood, and cover large and varied terrains. 'Fleas', wrote

* 'Very often and quite without fear it darted all over Aminte, right up to the precincts of love.'

Landor, 'know not whether they are upon the body of a giant or upon one of ordinary stature.' They know even less than that. The ways they tread, clawing a discreet path with their backward-pointed bristles for support, are plains of plenty, turning with the curve of their earth. They broach the light savannah of arm or leg, swathed preferably in the darkness of cuff, sleeve or trouser. A ticklish trail leads to vales and gullies of fleshy folds, to dark and tangled forest, to the gleaming white of high plateaux and the broad dividing canyons; across arid patches of callosity, skirting the hillocks of spot, mole and carbuncle, through groves and meadows of flock, flue and down, along the humped range of the spine from shadowy coccyx to the pinnacle of occiput. Always there is the ultimate sanction, the threat from those probing aerial pincers of thumb- and finger-nail, the swift whisking from hideaway to the dazzling brightness of execution, the clamp and cut of ungual guillotine, or life squeezed out through a constricting choke.

All the same, fleas in this line encounter less hazards than might be expected. They are the spectators, important as such, and as often as not they tell the story themselves. They are not the best raconteurs, given much to pun and vulgarism and seldom able to distil eroticism from the blatant catalogue of acts. So the *Autobiography of a Flea* (a tale claimed to have been published in 1789, more likely a century later, in a limited edition of 150 copies) is thus introduced:

> Told in a Hop, Skip and Jump, and recounting all experiences of the Human, and Superhuman, Kind, both Male and Female; with his Curious Connections, Back-bitings, and Tickling Touches; the whole scratched to-gether and arranged for the Delectation of the Delicate, and for the Information of the Inquisitive, etc., etc., Published by the authority of the Phlebotomical Society.

The tale unfolds after a clumsy and ribald piece of doggerel. 'I was engaged', begins the flea narrator, 'upon professional business connected with the plump white leg of a young lady of some fourteen years of age.' This on Sunday, and in church. After the service, in the gloom of the cemetery, Bella, the young lady, is forcibly apprised of something she understood not at all before. Charlie is her instructor, but the coaching soon falls to Father Ambrose, who silently witnessed the first lesson, and appropriates the function on the threat of informing Bella's father. In the manner of that hermit from Boccaccio who showed an aspirant maiden how to admit the devil to hell, Father Ambrose instructs Bella in the righteous task of relieving a poor cleric's tensions. She acquiesces, and performs a series of unusual operations on him to his very great delight.

This interlude, in turn, has been watched through a key-hole by Brother Clement and the Father Superior, who now appear on the scene to enjoy and vary their colleague's recipe. 'Anyone would have supposed', remarks the flea, 'that a flea of average intelligence only would have had enough of such exhibitions as I have thought it my duty to disclose; but a certain feeling of friendship as well as sympathy for the young Bella impelled me still to remain in her company.' His stay reveals more quirks of his provident species. More clerics are conscripted, as well as 'a titled lady' arrived for confession. After fifty pages or so the epithets assume a certain monotony, chosen as they are to emphasise enormity and vigour. After a hundred, the description of a most ordinary transaction, spreading over twenty pages, induces yawns in the reader, though not in the participants, long before its natural resolution. In the end, both Bella and her friend Julia take the veil, a ritual followed by the hearty celebrations of a host of novices and more experienced interns. All of which proves too much for the flea, who emigrates. The book is in that class of works known as anti-clerical.

It is typical. There are other autobiographies, and some memoirs, and a host of reminiscences, all by fleas. There are tales about fleas, tales with mentions of inquisitive fleas, and accounts of the exploits of downright prurient fleas. From time to time fleas play a part in the rituals and experiments. Among gatherings of the lower orders their familiar presence enhances the piquancy of sensation. Sometimes it spoils it. At the sight of the more *outré* procedures of the human pantomime, their hearts leap, electric thrills pervade their anomalous marrows, they cry for joy, or leap in ecstasy. Sometimes, as noted, they press home their spiky goads, always into those soft and sensitive parts with which they, far more than the actual owners, are familiar, in order to stifle some vile stratagem. They are generally on the side of right and the moral code, though they are known to yield to jealousy.

Once or twice they are put to most original use. In *Miss High-heels*, a work published in Paris (in a green cover and in English) in 1931, they function in their weirdest role. It is the pitiful saga of Dennis, a rich and epicene young man under the control—and often, to his perverse pleasure, under the rod —of his tautly beautiful step-sister and her aunt. Dennis, of course, is incorrigible, but the ladies persist. They search their minds for fresh methods of correction, and do not neglect the tried ways of icy abuse, spirited spanking and exposed confinement in constricting bonds. Now and again they devise a breakthrough. In one of these, large glass containers full of brown dust are clamped to the hero's hands and feet. The dust, he and we discover without overdue surprise, is nothing but captive swarms of fleas.

Where bawdy is concerned the prolific German output appears to lack two qualities, humour and happiness. There is no sharing of that sensual connoisseurship that spanned the age between the *Decameron* and *Fanny Hill*. The want is made good by profusion. Germans—I have it on hearsay—are sexual gourmands and those of them who chronicle the mechanics of love record a long sustaining of crescendo. There is little comic or facetious or slanted or wry or tendentious or understated. There is instead the clash of bodies, the lusty smack of flesh against flesh, the avid mating-cry, the echoing decibels of Teutonic union. Even perversities lose their arcane appeal when the thwack of leathern thong, the clamorous vulgarity of black strap and bodice, and forbidden minglings of man with man, woman with woman, resound indistinctly in the raucous pageant. Still, through it all, the small voice of the flea comes through clear and persistent.

Nothing suggests the German people are more infested with fleas than other races. On the contrary. Their pornography, however, is. Fleas are so much a German erotic speciality that two learned Teutons, Herren Hugo Hayn and Alfred N. Gotendorf, applied themselves at the turn of the century to compiling a bibliography of the literature. *Floh-Litteratur,* they called it, *des In- und Auslandes vom xvi. Jahrhundert bis zur Neuzeit.** The bulk of works listed and sometimes briefly and drily appraised ('a cultivated recital'; 'curious anecdotes'; 'indelicate matter') is German, though English and French achievement is duly recorded too.

Despite the skill and labour of this industrious pair, the chase they initiated brings little reward. The works listed are spread and treasured through the state collections of Europe. They include satire, venomous quills aimed at things and people long forgotten, transient gossip whose objects are as unknown as village Hampdens. There are stylistic curiosities (the oldest German macaronic poem in hexameters); some turns of wit:

> *Ce git, qui prenant ses ébats*
> *Sur le corps délicat d'une gente femelle,*
> *Par un faveur rare et belle,*
> *Au milieu des plaisirs y trouva son trépas.†*

and endless punning on the French word for flea (*puce*) and that for virginity (*pucelage*).

---

* *German and Foreign Flea Literature from the 16th Century to the Present Day.*

† 'Here he lies who, revelling in a sweet maid's tender body, met his end— through a favour of rare delight—in the midst of pleasure.'

Yet for all their diversity of title and language, the scope of erotic contents is foreseeably confined. A nubile maid—Barbara, Anna, Yvette or another of the faceless parade—frets at a flea tickle. She calls a servant to trace the vandal.

Illustration from a mildly erotic nineteenth-century novelette, *La Puce*, in which the flea plays a useful and typical part

Disarray is advanced when her lover arrives, breaks impetuous into the room, retires gawky at his offence. But Yvette in cool cunning sends the servant away and coyly invites the new-comer to resume the hunt; and the skeins of plot join at fervid clutch, buss and tup, sure as homing bees meet at the hive. And there are other themes; flea as scribe to a licentious court, reporting from the front of lechery, flea as first cause, as initiator of itch and fidget and ticklish desire, as malevolent creation of wilful gods. No new thing under the sun. It takes more than a flea to staunch an apocalypse.

Many of these works are illustrated. There is in fact a whole class of erotic flea art, but what is legal lacks distinction and what is distinct lacks legality. Bodies, however lascivious, take on the repulsiveness of skin disease when mottled with a flock of fleas. Even one is a blemish that repels, stemming titillation. Besides, the treatments are on a level with the stories. The twentieth century needs wrier stimulants. The gentleman whose original commission led to the painting of Fragonard's *The Swing* paid, and was happy to pay, for his own inclusion 'in a position to observe the legs of this charming girl'. His modern counterpart would invest differently. Aphrodisiacs, as physical mysteries recede, need to be more cerebral. There is little cerebral or aphrodisiac about classical figures cautiously undraped, still less when the overt purpose is a quest for vermin. Nor do the other fantasies succeed where this fails.

Flea pornography is aptly a microcosm of pornography in general. It offers a deal of indecent exposure without striking revelation. For centuries, however, it occupied the fabled flea, made it aware of human traits and frailty. It is a chapter in the flea biography, and the chapter is done.

5

PERFORMING FLEAS

One made a Golden Chain with lock and key,
And four and twenty links drawn by a flea,
The which a Countess in a box kept warm,
And fed it daily on a milk-white arm.

JACK DONNE *filius*

Perhaps it began with a human wish to be god, and so to control a community. It may have been mere three-dimensional doodling. At some stage, and somewhere, a nameless creator saw the potential for human amusement in a flea. Nowadays the scarcity of fleas among those with time or urge to develop this use has caused the tradition to subside. All the same, it had a long and varied run.

Flea circuses were but a part of the practice. It was not only amid the gaudy blare of the fair that fleas played their varied parts of pet, mimic and martyr. In Mexico, it seems, the Church has long been patron of the flea arts. There, incarcerated nuns, with minds keen as their fellows' but far less to make of them, took long ago to creating miniatures, pinhead models of the various sights they knew. Instead of modelling microscopic people, they found ready-made models in the insect world. Nimble fingers tired and eyes deteriorated as they clothed the corpses of fleas in elaborate costumes. Unconsecrated ladies took up the art and found they could make a little profit selling these *pulgas vestidas* as souvenirs. They set their children to catching the creatures from dogs, cats and themselves, and silently worked in the evenings on the daily bag. Dressed-up fleas are still sold among the indigent majority of Mexican people. Two specimens on display at

Tring show a male in a white suit and white floppy hat, with a bundle of sticks on his back. Only his head and feet are visible. His wife wears a crimson dress and white pinafore and carries a pink jug. Both are displayed under a magnifying glass. A more elaborate exhibition is on show at the Museum of Childhood in Edinburgh. There a company of flea corpses has been wrought into the semblance of a wedding.

There are records of fleas being kept as pets, suspect per-haps from the point of view of the owner's affections as much as the volatility of the insects. Nevertheless, among others it is told that Willughby, a friend of the naturalist John Ray, gave bed and board to a favourite flea, admitting it at certain times to suck the palm of his hand. After three months of com-patibility the flea died of cold, occasioning more than due grief. But it was left to the hardy Christina of Sweden, in a life busy with intrigue and virile exploits, to devise the strangest employment. She amused herself by executing fleas, as it is said she enjoyed the torments of human transgressors. To this day a small gun, four inches long, is exhibited in the arsenal at Stockholm—a piece of Lilliputian artillery made expressly for her flea-slaughter.*

The idea of the flea circus seems to have been English. That at least was the verdict of the sixteenth-century English writer Thomas Moufet. He wrote that fleas have 'a little head, and a mouth not forked but strong and brawny, with a very short neck, to which one *Mark* an *Englishman* (most skilfull in all curious work) fast'ned a Chain of Gold as long as a mans finger, with a lock and key so rarely and cunningly, that the Flea could easily go and draw them, yet the Flea, the Chain,

* The Arsenal authorities say the gun was used simply for courteous games with the Queen's noblemen. Evidence for the flea connection comes from Linnaeus. The Lapps, he wrote in *Lachesis Lapponica*, destroy lice with their nails, 'these people having no firelock to shoot them with'. A nineteenth-century editor of the book, J. E. Smith, said the allusion was to: 'a little gun, four or five inches long, still shown in the Arsenal at Stockholm, with which vulgar report says the famous Queen Christina used to kill fleas'.

lock and key were not all above a grain weight'. Moufet had heard 'from men of credit, that this Flea so tied with a Chain, did draw a Coach of Gold that was every way perfect, and that very lightly; which much sets forth the Artists skill, and the Fleas strength'.

Mark comes through to us as something of a medieval sorcerer, putting aside potions and the philosopher's stone to create pageantry of golden gossamer. It was much later that regimenting fleas became a side-show in fair and market. It was not until the eighteen-thirties that the flair and devotion of Signor Bertolotto raised show-business fleas to the level of stardom.

'Extraordinary Exhibition of the Industrious Fleas', Signor Bertolotto announced, with usual éclat listing as patrons those minor lights of European royalty who, washed into England by tides of revolution, sought any setting where they might glimmer still. The show, in one poster that has survived, is placed at the Cosmorama Rooms, 209 Regent Street (now the rebuilt Polytechnic Institute), and an unabated concourse of visitors' had determined the impresario to keep it open a few weeks more. 'Any comment on the merit of this Exhibition would be useless; the unparalleled success it has obtained during the last two years is sufficient proof that it deserves (as it has obtained) the public patronage.' Signor Bertolotto anti-cipated the century of publicity. And charged one shilling admission.

He took immense interest in his subject. He wrote a book to which this one is in some respects in debt, which drew lavishly on his own experience and perhaps more reliably on the current *Encyclopaedia Britannica*. 'By constant practice,' he writes, 'I know my own fleas as a shepherd knows his cattle.' Nor does he omit that many of his flock have been fed by 'ladies of distinction'. His flair, his Italian brio and sense of style and occasion come through well, a masterful master of ceremonies. No wonder the gentry and unseated monarchs flocked to the show.

UNDER THE PATRONAGE OF HER

Royal Highness the Princess Augusta

THE

NOBILITY, GENTRY, &c.

A

PROGRAMME

OF THE

Extraordinary Exhibition

OF THE

INDUSTRIOUS FLEAS,

BEING CONSIDERED ONE OF THE

Greatest Natural Curiosities

EVER EXHIBITED.

Title-page from the programme for Signor Bertolotto's Regent
Street Flea Circus in the 1830's

Sadly, the Signor and his show are gone. All that remains are the programme notes; of a ball at which flea ladies partner their frock-coated gentlemen, and a twelve-piece flea orchestra plays audible flea music, while in an alcove four whiskery old flea bachelors make up a four at whist. Another scene, a mail coach and coachman in the royal flea livery, belabouring his four flea chestnuts with an actually cracking whip. Fanfares, and a Man of War is drawn on: a hundred and twenty guns, and the whole lifelike miniature drawn by a single flea,

A First-Rate MAN of WAR, 120 Guns.

DRAWN BY A SINGLE FLEA.

though the tableau is four hundred times it weight. Then the Great Mogul, complete with harem, a splendid palanquin, and a hookah at which he realistically puffs. Finally, the grand climax. A hush; and then enter accurate portrayals of the three heroes of Waterloo—Wellington, Napoleon and Blücher —three immortal miniature warriors. It was they and Bertolotto who brought the flea circus to its apogee.

While Bertolotto created midget accoutrements for his performers, others could reproduce the flea itself, life-size. A story about this was told by Nikita Krushchev, Russia's prime minister, when he visited England. In the nineteenth century, he told his audience, the King of England, in order to vaunt his people's skills, had a perfect life-size model of a flea made

Napoleon on his Charger.

and sent to the Czar of Russia. The Czar, not to be outdone, passed it on to a Russian craftsman with orders to make one as good. In due course the man arrived at the Kremlin and presented the flea—with boots on. 'But it's the same flea,' exclaimed the Czar. 'No, no,' protested the craftsman, 'it has boots on.'' And nowadays,' said Krushchev, 'the saying in Russia is, when we want to boast of our great craftsmanship: "The Russian craftsman puts on the shoes of the English flea".'

For a hundred years after Bertolotto the flea circus showed canny vigour in surviving. At the present day, those above a certain age remember the show as a commonplace of their early outings and treats. For them it had the added curiosity of being a daily menace brought to the limelight—the ugly sisters' vision of Cinderella. Most towns of Europe and America had a resident or itinerant trainer with his booth, his outrageous claims, his hopping troupe. More recently they have been hard hit by hygiene, change of taste and especially slum clearance. Ten years ago one could be found among the side-shows of most big fairs and circuses. But in frantic quest the trainers were already offering a pound for twelve fleas. Now, only one survives in England, and that leanly; three are known in France. In the United States the famous flea circus at Hubert's Museum near Times Square in New York has been closed for fifteen years. There are a few scattered across the country, but hygiene relentlessly kills off human fleas —the only ones with the necessary jumping power.

Professor Len Tomlin maintains, or tries to maintain, his dying craft amid the popcorn vulgarity of Manchester's Belle-vue Park. There, a little to the left as you go in, a round booth encloses the table, which is the fleas' stage, and a few chairs for the audience. Outside a notice announces POSITIFLEA AN ALL LIVE SHOW. Bertolotto would have recoiled in Latin swoon but Professor Tomlin (the prefix is traditional, if not academic) brings the skill of a trained jeweller to the creation of his tableaux. Only three men in the world, he is reported as saying, have the steadiness of eye and hand to harness fleas. The acts he creates include a fencing match between Pedro and Pierro, a ballet sequence, a tightrope walk, a roundabout and a chariot procession. The skill and variety, he claims, are due to his twenty-four years of experience.

Nevertheless, Professor Tomlin's dedication will not turn the tide. With the field to himself, he still cannot find enough fleas. Suppliers vanish. Once, in Hull, he saw 'a likely-looking family', followed them home, and made his strange request for livestock. After that the husband sent him twelve recruits whenever he received a cheque for a pound. They went by post and the Professor collected them at the post office next morning. For raw flea recruits, postal confinement was perhaps a suitable initiation. But that contact went away. He was suc-ceeded by an old-age pensioner couple in Manchester. Slum clearance dried up the source, pitching his suppliers into cleanly apartments anathema to fleas. People don't even sleep on straw mattresses any more. The result is sad. Whole bank-holiday weekends go by without the Professor being able to open the box office. He would have nothing to show if he did.

What in fact he and his colleagues are selling is a matter for some debate. Without slurring the fleas themselves so much as those who purport to train them, it has been said, by more than one expert, that this whole delicate business is a matter of per-fect simplicity. True, wrapping silver wires the width of hair round the necks of fleas requires a steady hand and a good eye. But many deny any need of training. The minute harness en-sures perfect discipline. The flea goes and comes as he is prompted by a tug or a push, and the power of his back legs, used normally for titanic leaps and now constrained by fetters, becomes a controlled piston quite capable of drawing heavy weights. The insect's stamina is also phenomenal. It is capable of performing in fifty ten-minute shows a day, and continuing thus for a fortnight or more.

Even worse, according to the late Harold Russell, is the basic preparation, a straight crib from the old days of slavery. The fleas, he wrote, are put in a glass which acts as the equiva-lent of a treadmill. Here they learn, through laborious ex-perience, that their faculty for jumping no longer gets them anywhere. From then on, what is paraded as the result of skill and learning is a hamstrung urge to escape. Cement is used liberally, to stick fleas to the orchestra seats, or to each other in a semblance of dancing, or swords to their legs. The rest is the result of chance and control. Ballets, duels and gala coaches owe such conviction as they elicit to glue and lifelong tether-ing. Only at the end, when the acts are over, is there a touch of spontaneity. The trainer rolls back his sleeve and invites the performers to feed. To the fascination of young spectators they do so. But this, of course, is no act. After their exertions the fleas are hungry.

Bertolotto would doubtless have flared at such charges. He would have defended his art. He believed in understanding his fleas, and if he knew less than the whole truth about their physiology, he claimed to know their minds. 'Fleas', he wrote, 'are particularly of an obstinate disposition; some of them will carry their stubbornness to such a pitch when in chains that they will not move a step, nor will they take any kind of food in spite of all my endeavours to make them. They will contract their legs and remain motionless as long as they think they are observed, and generally die in five or six days, victims to their obstinacy.'

There is little one could have told Bertolotto of his trade. Like Larry Adler with the mouth organ, he raised a knack to the level of art. If it dropped back as soon as he retired, the florid expatriate is the last to blame.

6

FACT FINDERS AND FANCIERS

Pulex, a flea (deriv. pulvis, dust)
LATIN DICTIONARY

Fleas, thought the Romans, were animated dust or dirt. Pliny the Elder, their greatest naturalist, wrote that some insects 'are engendered by filth, acted upon by the rays of the sun. These fleas are called "leapers" from the activity they display in their back legs. Others again are produced with wings, from the moist dust that is found lying in holes and corners.'

The Hebrews knew better. A clause in the Jewish *Talmud* orders that the flea, 'being one of the animals that propagate by copulation, is therefore not to be killed on the Sabbath'. But the dust theory, or something like it, persisted to modern times, solemnised by the title 'the theory of spontaneous generation'. Since it went on so long, and acted as catalyst to induce some major scientific discoveries and finally to unmask the flea's most villainous role, it is worth expanding a little. Observant men had always noticed that a good many minuscule animals lived in dust and mud, rotting timber and dead plants, in dung, swamp and urine. Many of these creatures seemed activated by the heat of the sun, and it came to be held that much life was started, not by usual reproductive processes, but as a result of heat and decomposition. Virgil, in the *Georgics,* showed the spontaneous growth of bees from the rotting carcass of a calf. Virgil and Pliny expressed the educated Roman view, and for a thousand and more years there was no discovery to change it. Variations were introduced to the theme, but in the main the Dark and Middle Ages were times of biological paralysis.

Sand, the dung of pigeons, the urine of men or goats, beads of sweat dropped from the brows of Negro slaves—these and more were specified, from time to time, as first causes. And when the light of the Renaissance dawned, still there was Van Helmont issuing instructions for the creation of mice from rags and wheat grains; and Francis Bacon himself reporting that fleas bred principally from straw or mats. Fleas' 'first Originall is from dust', wrote Moufet in the sixteenth century, 'chiefly that which is moyst'ned with mans or Goats urine. Also they breed amongst Dogs hair. . . .'

The seventeenth century, aided by lenses and imagination, did away with much of the hokum. But to break new ground it was necessary to crack the obstinate spirit of the clerical Middle Ages, a slow and heretical business that aroused the Inquisition's effective ire. Bad enough to revert to Aristotle, and throw off the mystical and mythical accumulation of the age of scholastics. Even worse to look beyond him.

For a thousand years the next world had been infinitely more important than this one, and of much more interest to the Cath-olic hierarchy. What it was necessary to know of the earth was duly revealed by heaven to a church that claimed absolute authority. The only concession was to Aristotle, whose books, it was stated, contained the sum of knowledge about nature. Those who relied on their own senses too much were locked up, like Roger Bacon, for 'suspected novelties'. But two hundred years and more after Bacon's death, he was followed by a grow-ing army that would not be denied. It had its martyrs—Vesa-lius and Galileo—but by the seventeenth century the force of naturalism held its own with supernaturalism in large areas of Europe. The seeds were sown of the empire of science, and shibboleths dropped like ninepins.

Academies of science sprang up—in Italy, France and Eng-land—in defiance of the clerical reaction of universities. The invention of microscope, telescope, barometer, thermometer, air pump and pendulum clock precipitated the scientific revolu-

tion. Among these the microscope and a series of notable exploiters of it enabled insects to be sketched on the rational map
of life. As early as 1610 Galileo, with perhaps the first primitive
microscope, discovered that some insects had compound eyes.
A little later Francisco Stelluti was describing the anatomy of
bees from minute observation. Marcello Malpighi a little later
wrote details of the heart of the bee at work, and contrived to
end his life as physician to a pope. Francesco Redi managed
to fit into the busy life of a Renaissance dilettante the study of
insect generation.

Before the turn of the seventeenth century those who kept
their eyes open could see that the flea, with all its six-legged
cousins, was a viable animal with as regular and vital a life
cycle as that of man himself. About this time the Netherlands
were enjoying their golden age, and fitly produced two of the
greatest names in early biology. With painstaking accuracy Jan
Swammerdam traced, from his own observation and with a
touching humility ('I do not know, for instance, what is the use
of the plume attached to the first pair of gills') the mysterious
life cycle of the mayfly. But in the matter of fleas, pride of place
goes to that ebullient surveyor of the minute, the Dutchman
Antoni van Leeuwenhoek.

Leeuwenhoek's microscopes—he made over four hundred
and jealously guarded them, prohibiting even friends from
using the best—comprised two tiny lenses which, in line with
the eye, magnified up to 270 times a minuscule portion of the
flea beneath. A little while before Robert Hooke had claimed
that 'the microscope is able to make no greater discoveries of the
flea than the naked eye'. But Leeuwenhoek was able, not only
to describe a flea, but the mite that was parasitic on its pupa.*
He showed equal spirit in describing a creature 'endowed with
as great perfection in its kind as any large animal' as in attacking

---

* Swift's lines on p. 108 were inspired by this discovery. Leeuwenhoek's
researches became so well known that the microscope was linked with the flea,
and known for long as a 'flea-glass'.

the conventional attitudes towards this 'minute and despised creature'. Chief among the philistines were those who still supported the theory of Spontaneous Generation, seeing the flea as a scion of dust, dung, scurf or sweat. To refute them, he kept and recorded a long watch on his charges.

> 6 July Worm came out of egg. 17 July Worm appeared all over white . . . spinning round itself a web or covering. 21 July . . . changed into an aurelia or chrysalis . . . of trans/ parent white . . . 25 July . . . assumed somewhat of a red colour . . . grew deeper and deeper . . . 30 July . . . entirely red, and in the evening the Flea it contained was leaping about in the glass.

In such a way he traced out the whole history of the flea's meta/ morphoses. 'Fleas', he concluded, 'are not produced from cor/ ruption, but in the ordinary way of generation.'

Leeuwenhoek's discoveries, on fleas, on circulation in eels and fish, on parthenogenesis among aphids, on ants' lives and spiders' venom, were described by him in letters sent to the Royal Society in London. The accounts were widely circu/ lated and greatly respected. Still, dead tenets refused to droop. Devout men of a literalist turn clung to Spontaneous Genera/ tion as to the Book of Genesis. In 1699 the same Royal Society found it necessary to publish a letter concerning the work of an Italian by the quaint name of Hyacinth Cestone. For new pebbles on the shore of scientific knowledge were for ever being obscured by the flowing of the tide of reaction, and Leeuwen/ hoek had failed to convince all. The letter was devoted to 'A New Discovery of, the Original of Fleas, made by the Signior D'iacinto Cestone of Leghorn'.

> At last [it runs] is discovered, by the indefatigable Industry of Signior D'iacinto Cestone, the true way of the Generation of fleas, their Worms, and entire Metamorphoses which have been hitherto obscure, though sought after . . . [While

claiming more than his due, the Signior coined his revela
tions in delicate prose. Fleas' eggs, he found] slip ordinarily
streight to the Ground, or fix themselves in the Plyes or other
inequalities of the Coverlets and Cloaths. From these are
brought forth white Worms, of a shining Pearl Colour,
which feed themselves on the Brann-like substance which
sticks in the Combs when Puppies are combed to take out
the Fleas; or with certain Downy substance that is found in
the Flyes of Linnen Drawers, or other such like Excrement.
They . . . are very lively and active, and if they have any
Fear, or if they be touched, they suddenly roul themselves up,
and make as it were a Ball. . . . When they are come to their
usual Bigness they hide themselves the most they can, and
bringing out of their Mouths the Silk, they make round
themselves a Small Bag, white within as Paper, but without
always durty and foul'd with Dust. . . . Two Days before it
comes out, it becomes coloured, grows hard and gets
Strength, so that coming speedily out, it streight leaps away.

By the end of the seventeenth century, fleas were more or less
accepted, not as wraiths or ordure, but as insects, and so ani
mals, in their own reproductive right. But not by all. Leeuwen
hoek and his predecessors had been the beacons of their own
remarkable century, like Newton, Pepys, Locke, Wren and
Vanbrugh in other lines, but not harbingers of a new enlighten
ment, whatever labels have since been pinned to the eighteenth
century. That second Augustan age ratified but the first stage of
Renaissance—the reversion to classicism. The concern of the
Englishman was physical and mental comfort, the rationalising
of past ups and downs into a level plain, a walk through which
would never upset the digestion. Borders, whether of know
ledge or territory, should stay if possible where they were, or
otherwise be reduced, like those of the first British empire. Sur
veying mankind from China to Peru taught rational men the
lesson learned painfully by Candide and Rasselas, that staying

home was the wisest policy. Academic exploration stood still. In this century—in some ways the Middle Ages of modern times—Spontaneous Generation once more flourished. It became a rallying cry for reaction, like monarchy, the birch and absence of income tax.

Moreover, nothing was done with knowledge gained earlier. The flea had been seen, recorded and ticked, and the matter was closed. Nobody tried to scrutinise its role in the general order of things. Bites and itching were well enough known, and there were sufficient remedies to make further research futile. For a hundred or so years, cultivated men, having reached a broad and fertile ledge on the long climb to knowledge, were content to relax and enjoy it. When the next impetus came, they bolted upwards at an unprecedented rate.

Spontaneous Generation was not dealt its death blow till the present century. But Pasteur bruised it badly a hundred years ago and there were others to follow him. Their stimulus came from the menace of disease among the growing populations of new towns, then beginning to snake into country/side, spreading a trail of cement and mortar that stifled the aspirations of grass, flowers and trees. Disease must be contained, to avert grave threats to life and progress. To this end, the theories about life being created from putrescence and miasma must yield.

The progressive belief was that all living things, however tiny, had a regular breeding cycle. From this, the theory, or hope, grew that disease itself was the work of microscopic but living things acting on and inside man and animals, and that by closer understanding of these minute organisms it would be possible to destroy them. Pasteur and others, to make an answer practicable, put the question this way. If harmful microbes infecting wine, milk and other commodities were produced through the mating of their parents, then violent heating of these liquids in sealed conditions would kill off the microbes and indefinitely free the liquids from contagion. But if Spontaneous Generation were true, no amount of boiling would

Flea circus at Bellevue Park, Manchester, possibly the only one left in Britain, run—when he can catch enough fleas—by 'Professor' Tomlin

One of the posters outside

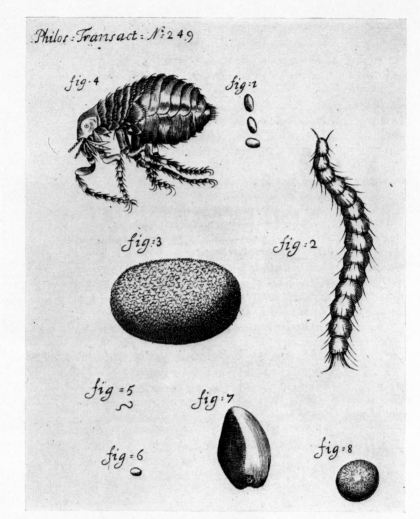

Stages of a flea's growth—egg, larva and pupa—from *Philosophical Transactions of the Royal Society*, No. 249, 1699

prevent more microbes from appearing and infecting the liquids. The logic was not foolproof, but it was a working postulate. Aided by the findings of Robert Koch and others, Pasteur heated his liquids and rendered them sterile, so proving to the satisfaction of many that his arguments were right. It was about the time that Darwin was decimating another flank of reaction. Medical science leapt for the first time out of sight of Galen, Hippocrates and Aristotle.

Spontaneous Generation began to lose its appeal. Deep-set ideas of impalpable vapours, hazy miasmata and the wrath of God gave way to a search for living microbes that caused disease. Pasteur was only part of a world-wide enlightenment. The idea of germs, or seeds of disease, being spread by some means of contagion went back five hundred years, was even mooted by the Greeks. But it was the nineteenth century that established and proved the thesis. Improvements in the micro-scope spurred progress. Then followed in quick succession the discoveries that yeast was a microscopic plant causing fermen-tation by its natural life cycle; and that a protozoan microbe caused a blighting disease in silkworms. As a result of all these advances, Koch and his associates isolated the organisms that bring about cholera, diphtheria and tuberculosis.

To some extent disease had been pinned down and given substance. But a debate remained and continued to rage on the means by which bacteria were conveyed from one species, and victim, to another. Some progress had been made in this direc-tion too. In 1877 it was shown that a blood disease, filariasis, was conveyed from man to man by mosquitoes. Soon after-wards the same insect's role in spreading malaria was suspected. In 1893, Theobald Smith contrived to show that Texas cattle fever was transmitted by ticks. The case against insects was accumulating.

Already, after Leeuwenhoek, those who bothered themselves about fleas had accepted that they did not arise from nothing, or worse, but by natural processes of reproduction. After medieval bastardy, fleas had been legitimised in the early days of the microscope. Then nothing happened. In the eighteenth century Linnaeus classified only two species of the insect and for most of the nineteenth the known number remained low. Fleas disgusted, and invited little enthusiasm. Gilbert White, reflecting the squeamishness of his age in *The Natural History of Selborne,* referred to fleas only once; and an editor a few years later felt the need to explain that sand-martin fleas, 'bed' fleas and swallow fleas were all different species. Pasteur and his fellows had more to do with bacteria and other microbes, to which a flea was a giant. A pesky parasite with a comic side to it—there was no good reason to examine its family tree. No reason that anyone knew.

At the end of the nineteenth century a number of things happened. Followers of Koch and Pasteur carried out investigations that seemed to incriminate fleas in an international strategy of destruction. World interest tremblingly focussed on an outbreak of disease in the Far East. English, French, Germans and Japanese began intensive research on the scene. The muddled campaign lasted about ten years; and at the end of that period fleas were exposed as one of the great ravagers of human life.

7

RAVAGES

> That evening, when Dr. Rieux was standing in the entrance, feeling for the latch-key in his pocket before starting up the stairs to his flat, he saw a big rat coming towards him from the dark end of the passage. It moved uncertainly, and its fur was sopping wet. The animal stopped and seemed to be trying to get its balance, moved forward again towards the doctor, halted again, then spun round on itself with a little squeal and fell on its side. Its mouth was slightly open and blood was spurting from it. After gazing at it for a moment the doctor went upstairs.

This is the beginning of Albert Camus' *The Plague. Mutatis mutandis*, it is the beginning of any outbreak of bubonic plague among men. It is important to remember that until the 1890's, the *fin de siècle* of Wilde, Beardsley and the Aesthetics, the cause of the disease was as mysterious as a divine sacrament. The death of a rat heralded the death of a million men. But nobody knew.

Bubonic plague is endemic in some parts of the world, which is to say that the plague bacilli exist in certain animals in certain regions without doing much harm. Above all they are to be found in marmots, susliks and some other rodents among the steppes of central and eastern Asia. Every so often these rodents come in close contact with hoards of rats, at times when either they or the rats set out on a periodic migration. It may then happen that fleas infesting marmots transfer by mistake or intent to rats, and stay with their new hosts.

Fleas are the main vectors of the disease. Feeding from an

infected marmot they suck up the bacilli. Some of these are passed to their new rat hosts. Other fleas carry more bacilli to other rats. Before long an epidemic is afoot among the rats and this is carried, again by the agency of fleas, to neighbouring communities of rats. After an interval the disease may spread from country rats to town rats. And there the human drama, like Camus' novel, opens.

Fleas like the blood they feed on to be at body temperature. As soon as the rat on which a rat flea is feeding dies, its body begins to cool. Instinctively, the flea looks for another rat. In normal times this is easily found. But in times of plague, rats are dying by the score and hundred, and an alternative canteen is not easily come by. In towns, however, there is a second choice of host; and in times of plague, therefore, fleas will sooner or later turn their attention to men. With them they bring those plague bacilli they have unwittingly ingested.

So the bacilli come to man himself. In its usual way the flea, safe landed on human flesh, walks a little, picks its plot, and punctures. A few bacilli pass from its mouthparts into the human bloodstream. It sucks, but its own gizzard is blocked with bacilli. It regurgitates the infected blood into the hole it has pricked. In a short while the flea, as much a victim as the mammals it lives off, dies of plague, starved through a block⁄ing mass of bacilli in its digestive system. Meanwhile man himself has caught bubonic plague.

The disease takes different forms in humans. In the main it incubates for about ten days before inducing its symptoms. These include the swelling of one gland, rarely more, usually in the groin (for which the Greek word is *bubon*), but some⁄times in the armpit, on the neck, or elsewhere. There is also a fever. The bubo may swell to the size of an orange. It then generally breaks and suppurates. Occasionally it disappears without any discharge. The mortality rate in most outbreaks is around eighty per cent. There are two similar diseases, septi⁄caemic plague and pneumonic plague, associated with bubonic plague. The first is an infection mainly of the bloodstream, and is likely to kill the victim within a few hours. Pneumonic plague is a complication of bubonic plague and pneumonia. It is caught through contagion, like influenza, and has a very high fatality rate.

Plague has probably brought more human grief and fear than any other single cause. It has also probably changed the course of history more than any other force.* This grief and history can, depending on our ideas of causality, be attributed to the flea. So also can a connected vein of fear, superstition, duplicity, exploitation, faith, heroism and intellectual wrangling that passes almost without break through the annals of the human species. The combined effects of Nero and Kubla Khan, of Napoleon and Hitler, all the Popes, all the Pharaohs, and all the incumbents of the Ottoman throne are as a puff of smoke against the typhoon blast of fleas' ravages through the ages.

The known outbreaks are numerous enough. Plague smote the Philistines, a Godsent punishment for stealing the Ark of the Covenant, and decimated the populations of Gath, Ashdod and Akron. It is better documented in the last two millennia, when three disastrous pandemics are on record. The first began in Justinian's Byzantium in the year 542. It lasted for sixty years and spread 'to the ends of the habitable world'. Gibbon thought it 'not wholly inadmissible' that a hundred million people were removed by it from the face of Europe. Rats on ships, though nobody knew it, spread the plague to every cosmopolitan port. Whether madness or disease were the first to appear cannot be known, but sure it is that the eastern empire in this time was mad. Tetchy and unscrupulous, Justinian sulked in his palace as his general Belisarius reconquered his western domains from the Goths, only to return to

* Historians generally overlook this aspect of history. For instance, it is not widely known that in 1918–1919 something like fifteen million people died of influenza, dwarfing the casualties of the war itself.

have his eyes burned out for a fictional insolence. Theodora, the empress, presided in the arcana of the palace over rituals of blood and lust dimly sketched for us by the court bio' grapher Procopius. In the big town itself, year in year out, Byzantine fought and massacred Byzantine in a riot of anarchy, according only to his arbitrary allegiance to the colour blue or green. At the heights of the plague (always in late summer) ten thousand people were dying each day and when, towards the end of the century, the menace withdrew, the Roman Empire was effectively destroyed and the Dark Ages began.

The lull that followed, though disease smouldered in Venice, Marseilles, the Levant and Persia, was a long one. Then in the fourteenth century, the ecology of microbes and susliks, rats and fleas, the invisible ripples of nature's whims across the steppes and mountains of the East, brought plague to Europe's threshold. Here man himself took an active part in the introduction. In 1346 a colony of Italian traders was besieged within the walls of Caffa, a Crimean trading town, by a marauding host of Tartars. The siege lasted three years. In the course of it plague broke out among the Tartars, killing thousands. Combining tactics with convenience the Tartars loaded the bodies of their dead on to catapults and fired them inside the city walls. When the siege was relieved one ship' load of Italians escaped to the Mediterranean. Days after their arrival in Genoa, symptoms of plague among the Genoese announced the commencement of the Black Death.

A few months spread it round Europe. The general estimate is that in three years a quarter of Europe's population was de' stroyed. The numbers in England and Italy were possibly halved. Without doubt, by disrupting the economies and politics of the continent, plague hastened the end of feudalism.

Black Death was a layman's label. The same pandemic of plague kept recurring for three hundred years, disappearing more or less with the trail of destruction over the City of London in 1665. In the hundred years before that, six outbreaks accounted for nearly a quarter of a million people in London alone.

During these three centuries the threat of plague was as commonplace as sudden changes of the weather. Scarlet-coated Wolsey went everywhere with an orange in his hand, 'filled with a sponge of vinegar or other confection against pestilent airs'. The court was forever moving to distant palaces as epidemics in the city threatened the royal inhabitants of Whitehall. Prevention was a lot better than all the alleged cures —which included running on five mornings, fasting and the advice 'ne use ne baths, ne sweate too much, all these openeth the pores of the body and maketh the venemous aires to enter'. Erasmus, fretting at the quality of his beer, wine and audiences at Cambridge, voiced a familiar caution when he said he would defer a coveted journey to London till frosts cleared the plague from it.

Exodus from the capital by land or river, long queues of packed barges or wagons, the rumble of carts for the dead, the filling of open pits used for burial at times of high mortality— all these were familiar in London. Frequent use of plague imagery in Shakespeare and others shows how fear of the disease was imprinted on men's minds:

> as a planetary plague, when Jove
> Will o'er some high-voiced city hang his poison
> In the sick air.

Strange beliefs grew and throve. Aerial spectres were seen in human shapes. The Plague Maiden appeared, a bright in-candescence in the sky scattering the seeds of disease, or as a mortal woman ordering a peasant to carry her on his shoulders as she spread the plague, with immunity as his reward. Arabs led through the streets camels which, having drawn the con-tagion upon themselves, were ceremonially strangled. In Mar-seilles a man would volunteer to be scapegoat. After a year of luxury and indulgence at the expense of the townsmen he was

duly stoned to death outside the walls, a Faustus of the plague.*
Hundreds, at the onset of the menace, turned to God and
piety. As many, despairing of long life, chose licence and
lechery for the short remainder. In Europe the icy zeal of the
Flagellants revived and crowds flogged their own skins that
would soon be hardening in the grave. Others looked to burden their enemies with the blame. In most Western countries
Jews were tortured, speared and burned in periodic pogroms
for putting magical plague concoctions in the holy water of
Christian churches, or in wells in common use.†

Every kind of formula, talisman, philtre, scarab and charm
was brought into use. People inscribed prayers and acrostics
(formations in which ABRACADABRA or SATAN-ADAM
could be read in different directions were popular) on stone
and wood and nut and amulet. Sapphires were held a pro-
tection against plague, and amber was the poor man's sapphire.
New meanings were read into the Bible and the texts of
medieval schoolmen. Comets and other omens were recalled
as having presaged plague outbreaks. Witchcraft, at its
strongest over those centuries, owed less to pagan precedents
than to the credible superstition of the age. To save themselves
from plague, the Stuarts smoked, and Pepys chewed, Raleigh's
new-found prophylactic tobacco. The boys at Eton were com-
pelled to smoke to save their skins. In London during the
great outbreak forty thousand dogs and five times as many cats
were killed as a sanitary precaution. But nobody thought about
fleas.

Then again the plague departed, without notice or cere-
mony. Again it lingered here and there, but in such proportions that Europe could forget. For two hundred years it made
little difference to Europeans. In the eighteenth century it

* A close equivalent of the original Jewish 'scapegoat', animals on which
high-priests laid the sins of the people, then exiled them to the wilderness.

† In India, in 1896, a typical rumour accused the English of putting snake-
venom in the Bombay water-supply, so causing the city's epidemic.

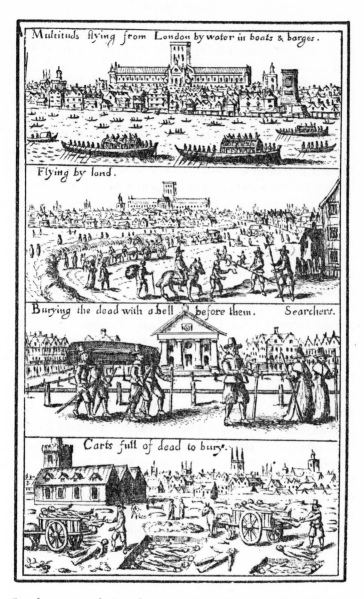

London scenes during the 1665 Great Plague, a contemporary print

confined itself without great virulence to Marseilles, Moscow, Sicily and the Middle East. By the mid-nineteenth century it had disappeared even from the Levant, after a final nibble costing the lives of 30,000 Cairenes in 1834. It still, however, held an atavistic horror. Catherine the Great and Napoleon (who touched the victims of it at Acre during his eastern campaign, to encourage his troops) had been among several sovereigns who forbade mention of the word. And at the Great Exhibition in Paris in 1889 there was talk of official bribery and even murder, put in chain to snuff out rumours of an outbreak, and so preserve the event's commercial value.

In 1878, news of a fresh outbreak at Astrakhan, by the mouth of the Volga, had taken complacent Europeans by surprise. Missions were sent hurriedly to report on the chances of its spread to the west. Almost before they had time to do so the scare had died down. Thirteen years later plague was reported from Hong Kong, in more serious strength, having arrived recently from Canton. Again experts were alerted. This time their interest and concern were maintained. For this was the beginning of the third great plague pandemic, which took a toll of thirteen million people across the world. From Hong Kong it passed to Bombay, and thence to other Indian provinces. Its severity increased. By 1903 there were over a million deaths a year from it in India alone. It crossed the water from Bombay to Java and Japan, and before long the trading vessels that docked in Bombay had brought it to Asia Minor, South Africa, Mediterranean Africa and west, central and southern America. Still it was fleas that carried it—fated though they were themselves—from rat to rat and from rat to man. And still, while panic and precaution mounted, nobody knew.

Fleas could not long escape the earnest attentions of scientists. Other insects were implicated in other diseases. As the track of plague was slowly pieced together, it became apparent that certain types of flea were always at the scene of the crime. This in itself was no proof. But the dossier was opened.

By the 'nineties a handful of researchers, collecting material gathered round the world, had described about seventy species of flea, a considerable advance on Linnaeus's two, though still no more than a fraction of the true number. In Germany, Julius Wagner, and in England, Nathaniel Charles Rothschild—second son of the first Baron, and a flea-collector only in his spare time—and Karl Jordan, his assistant, were pioneering the scientific study of fleas.* None of them directed his main interest toward disease. They advanced on a broad front.

But specialists were not lacking to begin investigations. They took ship to Bombay and other parts of the Far East to get first-hand evidence. It still took them ten years, while plague claimed its annual toll of a million in India, to reach firm conclusions, for the barriers they had to break through were more than scientific. They brought the methods, outlook and language of their respective countries, and often blurred issues by emotional disparity. Officialdom, knit in the British Indian Plague Commission, was fettered by official caution. Others were bound to prejudice by their religious precepts, or simply by believing what they had always chosen to believe and only sifting evidence likely to support it. The number of variables in the problem—possible means of catching the disease, the behaviour of different rodents, the number of insects present and the differences between species—made controlled experiment impossible. Only with great difficulty was a panicky public persuaded to help.†

* Rothschild, with his brother the second Baron, began the great collection at Tring, now one of the most active centres of flea research in the world.

† N. H. Swellengrebel, who later worked on plague in Java, described some besetting problems. For example, natives were paid to bring in rats found dead, for statistical use. Then, for convenience, the authorities asked only for rats' tails, done up in bundles of a hundred. After a while it was noticed that the inner tails in the bunches were man-made. A Chinese was manufacturing and selling them to natives. Everyone cleared a profit.

Some individuals worked consistently on the right lines against all odds. The plague bacillus itself was isolated. That done, it became possible to observe it both in rats and men, but it was essential to find how it passed from one to another. Contagious breath, said one strong school. An organic vector, said another. Among the latter the task was to correlate two lines of scientific observation—the presence of rat fleas (*Xenopsylla cheopis*, first found in Egypt and named after the builder of the first pyramid) in plenty at the scene of bubonic outbreaks, and the insects' suggested ability to pass plague bacilli from one host to another.

In 1898 a Japanese, Ogata, first outlined the part played by rat fleas in the transmission of the disease. It was a tentative theory. His findings were corroborated the following year by the Frenchman Simond. In 1904 Liston repeated and con/firmed the experiments. But officials doubted. They had too many theories to choose from.

Examination of the postulate was not helped by the little understanding of fleas and the frequent scarcity of rat fleas. But the idea made sense: rat to rat, rat to man, man to man, all through the common link of fleas. The Plague Commis/sion denied it. Their tests disproved it. But they were using the wrong species of flea.

Indians were still dying in millions, and the epidemic had spread. The crowded port of Bombay threatened the whole world. Most closely it menaced Australia, and in Sydney research was concentrated. Two years into the new century something approaching proof was emerging, accounting for all the conditions in which plague was found, and for such puzzles as its seasonal variation and the time it took, in apparent isolation from rats, to break out in men. Gradually the officials came round. Old ideas of infection gave way. By 1910 the Plague Commission had confirmed that fleas carried the disease from rats to men, and that without fleas it was impossible for the disease to be transmitted in large numbers.

A long scientific war, involving many great leaders and
several nations, had been resolved. Ironically, nature herself
had already relieved the scourge of India, and the crisis was
past.

But the ten years had not been wasted. Plague had spread
to other parts of the world and the pandemic continued for
years, fortunately confined more to rodents than men. Out of the
findings of that decade came a more thorough knowledge of
the plague, its components and behaviour; and the proba-
bility of being able to combat successfully a further serious
outbreak.

Out of it too came the doleful verdict: fleas were guilty to
the tips of their probosces. Doleful, because while they
offended they suffered in large numbers. For every man or rat
that ever died of plague, goes the estimate, at least ten times as
many fleas have similarly expired.

8

FLEAS PINNED DOWN

Elephants are always drawn smaller than life, but a flea
always larger.   DEAN SWIFT

A flea.

A pest, parasite, bloodsucker, goad, pygmy. A speck of
tobacco. A moralist, gallant, demon, Peeping Tom, circus
artiste. A mass murderer.

What is a flea?

A flea is a member of any of the nearly two thousand known
species of the order Siphonaptera, in the Endopterygote section
of the Neopterous division of the Pterygote subclass of the class
Insecta. It comprises a head, a thorax of three segments and
abdomen of ten.

The flea is an insect.

The currency of biological jargon is neither flattering nor
evocative. Three hundred years ago a scientist wrote of the flea's
'polish'd suit of sable Armour, neatly jointed, and beset with
multitudes of sharp pinns, shap'd almost like Porcupine's
Quills, or bright conical Steel-bodkins'. But the use of style by
men of science did not long outlive that of armour by the sol-
diery. Most fleas that end an analysed life in test-tube captivity
are given flat epitaphs in words too long for most of us. Poets,
on the other hand, turn to fleas, if they turn at all, in moods of
abandon, and sketch with the colours of whimsy. To have a
working picture of our villainous hero, it is necessary to steer a
middle course.

To most who have been aware of it, the flea is a potent and
elusive dot. Under the microscope the dot takes shape. Magnified twenty times, the prodigy of its working can be appreciated.

Leeuwenhoek, one of the first to inspect a flea under a microscope, employed an artist to sketch the images. After a while
the man looked up from his lens. 'Dear God,' he uttered,
'what wonders there are in so small a creature.'

Most of a flea's working life is spent creeping through forests
of animal fur or feathers. To this end it is created a great deal
taller than broad, as if it had been pressed hard on both sides.
In general shape it looks, from the side, like a long brown balloon that enlarges at the rear and is supported on the arched
backs of three bent and slender porters. The balloon is its body;
the porters its six legs. Its smooth shell is shiny, spread evenly
with back-projecting bristles, and divided into segments. Each
segment loosely overlaps the next and so allows the shell to curl
up or down, like that of a woodlouse or prawn. 'Fleas are not
lobsters, damn their souls,' remarked Sir Joseph Banks, but
they have surface similarities.

The flea is well streamlined. Neither neck nor waist divide
head from thorax or thorax from abdomen, as they do in most
other insects. The whole body is a smooth progression from
front to back. In photographs even the bristles look like those
rough strokes marked in cartoons to denote speed of movement.

The head of a flea is hard, smooth and aptly rounded or
pointed for clearing a way through furry undergrowth. It is
fitted with a precise array of feelers and stiletto suckers for the
surgical extraction of blood. There are two pairs of palps—
organs of touch—attached just under the front part of the head
and generally hanging down and slightly backwards. Behind
them are three stilettos, specialised mouthparts forming a proboscis for piercing and siphoning up blood. Beside these are the
maxillary shields, used for separating hairs and feathers and
clearing a way for the proboscis to do its work. A number of
fleas, but not all, possess eyes, one on each side of the head. In
species associated with diurnal hosts they are usually large, protruding and, to the devoted race of flea-fanciers, appealing.
'Very large and beautiful,' Signor Bertolotto called them. Some

species have a minute spiny comb on the head, and another, ruff-style, where the neck would be—both supposed to resist capture or dislodgement by the host. All have antennae, two of them, tucked in grooves behind the eyes; in the male they can spring out for a variety of uses. In the way of insects, the flea has no nose to breathe through, but a series of aerating vents along its body, a pair to each segment.

Behind the head comes the thorax, a sort of chest. Under each of its three segments a pair of legs is attached. The legs are gangling and ingeniously jointed. The largest pair is at the back and packs astonishing power for the leap. Each leg terminates in a pair of claws, effective for clinging, but making it difficult to walk on smooth surfaces.

The rear ten segments contain the main minutiae of the flea interior, the processes of breathing, circulating blood, digestion and what amounts—even disregarding the size of the beast—to the most elaborate sexual equipment in the world. External genitalia are confined to the eighth and ninth segments, while the tenth and last contains the anus.

Removed from the mental microscope, the flea falls back to size. Species vary, and the female of each is larger than the male. Individuals may swell a good deal during a meal. The largest known type, a North American giant, is eight millimetres long—about the length of a pencil's diameter. The female of the largest flea in Britain reaches six millimetres, but most are a good deal less than that. Nevertheless Signor Berto-lotto, who once discovered that eighteen of his performing fleas, of full growth, together and after a meal weighed one grain, could write so confidently that he knew his fleas as a shepherd knows his cattle. 'I could give each a name. I can tell whose turn it is to work.' Not lobsters, damn their souls, but individuals, to a flea.

† † †

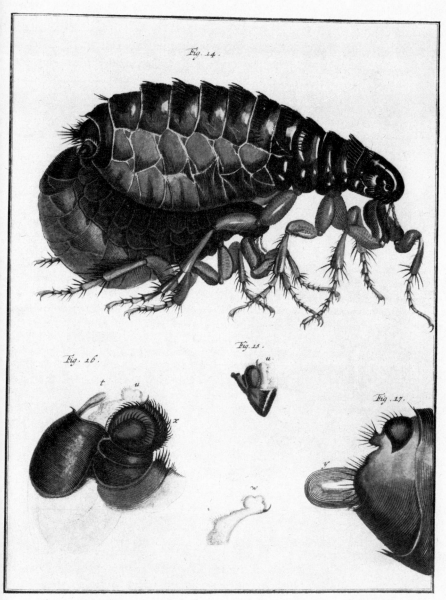

Fleas mating, from a remarkably accurate coloured German work, Roesel
von Rosenhof, *Sammlung der Mücken und Schnaken,* 1749.

A mouse flea seen through a microscope

The individual flea, like many other insects, becomes what it is through a process far different from human growth. Full-grown man has instantly recognisable similarities to his minutes-old offspring. The seven stages of man are an obvious evolution. The four of the flea are at first sight puzzlingly disparate. All the same, egg, larva and pupa are as essential to the develop-ment of the mature flea as infancy and adolescence to adult man. Life for the flea starts in the confines of an egg-shell, in most species about half a millimetre long, still large in comparison with the eggs of other insects. The eggs are pearly white, some-times rather darker, and if they lie on a contrasted surface can be seen by humans. The mother lays them, in small batches, on the host's body, on the floor of his nest, burrow, room, or in his bed. They normally hatch after a few days and sometimes a few weeks. By that time the embryo has developed into a miniature larva that breaks, with the help of a hard butt on its forehead, the case of its prison. It now embarks on the expansive phase.

If it is oddly common for the adult flea to elicit what almost amounts to affection in man, it is rationally rare for anyone to grow fond of the larval maggot. The sins of flea-youth, though far from harmful, are unforgiveable in human terms and the maggot, *qua* maggot, stands little chance of sympathy. In the course of its growth from one to as much as five millimetres, it leads a lurid life with callous brio. It wriggles its bristly pallor over the floor of room, sett, nest or den, feeding on the refuse of dried skin scratched or combed, all unaware, by its host. Equally necessary to its diet, in most cases, are the droppings of adult fleas, dried but undigested blood excreted during and after meals. By means of the iron in this blood, the larva begins to develop a hard cuticle that will finally become its shell. It will sometimes eat dead flies or gnats. For the rest, it grows and wriggles in an endless, legless, eyeless quest for food and stature. Disturbed, it rolls itself into a spiral. It has none of the boldness of its parents and is technically not a parasite. In the wrong con-ditions, without warmth, damp and gloom, it will die. But it has resources, once noted by that scrupulous observer, Berto-lotto. 'It is worthy of remark', he wrote, 'that if two of these little worms are enclosed in a narrow space, deprived of food, they will attack each other, and each taking hold with its mouth of its adversary's tail, so as to form a ring, will eat one another. This ring becoming smaller and smaller every day for five or six successive days, without either of them leaving their hold, they finally die, and becoming dry are sufficiently hard to be pre-served.' In better conditions the larval stage lasts two or three weeks. Thereafter the ingenious creature salivates a silky thread, doubles up in the shape of a ∪, spins a silk cocoon round itself, and remains in its wrap for its third, pupal, phase.

Metamorphoses is the word given to these various changes, but it is most apt for the pupal one. A maggot is a far cry from a fully-fashioned flea. The development is still wrapped in mystery, and in the soft and paper-thin case that conceals it, and most that is known is the surface truth. The pupa starts off white but darkens gradually. The cocoon is sticky and in a short time becomes camouflaged brown or grey by a coating of dust and dirt. So it remains for the week or two that the stage usually lasts, and at the end of that time a drowsy adult is wait-ing for release. Yet release may not come. Somewhere in the course of its evolution the flea grew tired of false entrances and devised a mechanism against too many repeats. Its first concern, on waking, will be a living source of food. To make this more likely the creature stays sleeping till nearby vibrations summon it to life. All unknowing, a man entering a long disused room, a bird returning after long absence to its nest, a badger plod-ding home from an extended outing—any of these may be the Prince Charming unwittingly kissing the drowsy succubus to consciousness. There is no hurry. The flea can stay alive and inactive over a year within the cocoon till its big chance comes. As soon as movement stimulates, the flea wakes, discards its soft coat, makes rapidly for the host, and commences adult life, a nourishing world of artesian wells at its hitherto unused feet.

In some ways it has been remarkable already, but no more than other arthropoids. Thousands of insects start life by moult, ing one stage to enter a new. Many maggots are agile and in, genious, and the caterpillar can be far more beautiful. Silk moth butterflies spin as fine a cocoon as fleas, and wood,borers are more ingenious over their emergence into the world. The flea so far has been true to his class, but not exceptional. From now on he is unique.

To narrow the field, the biography that follows is in most respects that of a human flea. More suitably known as *Pulex irritans* (irritating flea), it infests badgers and pigs more than humans and is nowadays losing ground on some human ter, ritories to cat fleas and dog fleas. But it is the star of the flea circus and will serve as a model. Its total world may be a room, a tent, a cave. But there is a universe outside, and a chance en, counter—a walk or plane,flight by its host, a companion in its host's bed, a mere dustpan and brush—may spatially translate it by astronautical dimensions. But if given the choice, and the ability to make one, it would probably opt for humble stability and the cultivating of one garden.

Its life span is not rigidly set. If everything went well it would probably survive about a year and a half. That would need an uncanny combination of correct temperature, correct food, supply, correct humidity, and a dozen other things. Nature is seldom so kind, and the adult flea may expect no more than two or three months of life. A rodent flea on record was known to last five years and thereby probably set up a freak record. A human flea in the laboratory has reached four hundred days. Signor Bertolotto wrote in 1834: 'I possess one nineteen months old, and to all appearance in the full enjoyment of all its physi, cal faculties.' Later he was able to record that it died of old age after twenty,three months: 'For the last two months it could not leap an inch high, crawling with great difficulty across its little box. As it grew weak I released it from the ten links of gold chain which had been constantly attached to it. It ate voraciously to the last, and was grown to such an incredible size as to be easily mistook for a bug.' But this was Methuselah. For most, a quarter of a year is the limit.

Into this time they fit, without hurry, the twin priorities of eating and breeding. A host is essential for both processes. So, as soon as possible after awakening, they make their first call on the nearest living creature. But even the confines of a small room or den are infinitely vast for the dimensions of a flea. Evolution has consequently awarded them a most magical set of senses to spot their prey, and a most potent means of locomotion to reach him without delay.

The eyes of a flea, where they exist at all, are weak. They can probably discern vague shadows and the rough shapes of things, but might not distinguish a man from his overcoat hanging on the door. It matters little, despite the satisfied verdict of the character described by Lucian:

> A blockhead, bit by fleas, put out the light,
> And chuckling cried, 'Now you can't see to bite'.

The flea is well compensated for poor eyesight. It can possibly hear. It can certainly smell, and uses the power to tell one potential host from another (there are fleas that would sooner die than suck from the wrong host). Smell is probably perceived by its fold-away antennae, or by the palps that hang down where, in human terms, its nose might be. These feelers, as well as the area of soft sensitivity called the *sensilium,* at the rear of its body, probably pick up other things too, currents of air, vibrations, degrees of warmth.

If little is known of the nature of flea senses, a good deal is recorded about their efficacy. When the lusty male approaches his mate he does so in a zigzag path as though minutely following a track of air, and some delicate scent exuded from her. There is no doubt fleas like warmth. To this day in parts of

Africa villagers put a lighted candle in a shallow dish of water in the middle of room or hut. Drawn by warmth, the flea leaps up and alights in a watery grave.

The awareness of vibrations which first called fleas out of their silky cocoons remains with them through life. They make for a movement, and often discover a source of blood. They can also distinguish between the chemical components of breath and so gauge the nature of a passing animal. With a tender equipment, sensitive to the slightest differences of noise, light, smell, vibrations, warmth, air currents and many other factors they have little trouble in deciding where to go.

An experiment was conducted to test both the senses and the travelling power of the rabbit flea, possibly one of the cleverest species in the world. Two hundred and seventy fleas were marked, then dropped at fairly regular intervals in a field of two thousand square yards. Then three rabbits were introduced, after the boundary had been sealed to prevent their escape. After a few days the rabbits were caught and examined. Between them, they were carrying just under half the total number of fleas released. So fleas, having sensed their prey, are very good at getting to it. For a human, pro rata, the distances to be covered would have seemed formidable, but fleas are extraordinarily well endowed for movement. They jump.

The problem of the flea's leap is not, one is aware, the most important in the world. Aristophanes, indeed, described the study of it as the most ludicrous of human occupations. In *The Clouds* he shows Socrates—in his opinion a vacuous mincer of words—and a young friend trying to establish how many of its own lengths a flea, at one spring, could hop. They make a wax impression of a flea's foot, and deduce from its measurement the length of a flea's body, on the principle *ex pede Herculem*. They then prod the flea to jump from Socrates' hand to his disciple's, record the distance, and by some complicated arithmetic arrive at an answer. To Aristophanes, a hemlock end likely seemed a just reward for such pettifoggery. But there are other points of view. Professor Arthur Ubbelohde, Head of Chemical Engineering at London University, put one recently: 'The electro-mechanical processes utilised by a hopping flea or buzzing mosquito are still immeasurably ahead of any modern power contrivance in the range of human inventors.' There, despite Aristophanes, seems reason enough to probe.

The answer to Socrates' problem is now known from more reliable observations. A human flea *can* jump about a hundred and fifty times its own length along, and about eighty times its length up. Its known record jump is eight inches high, twelve and a half along. (Its leg measures one-twentieth of an inch.) In human dimensions this would mean a man could top St Paul's Cathedral and cover a quarter of a mile without touching ground; but scientists smirk at the comparison and point to the neglect of such factors as weight and air resistance.

Hans Andersen's story about the flea at a jumping contest is related elsewhere. The spectators—perhaps the same crowd that was ready to see a resplendent regalia in the emperor's nudity—would not believe the flea jumped at all. In more than one respect, its leap is almost incredible. Simultaneously, the two middle segments of its hind legs extend with elastic rapidity. It bounds into the air and sometimes bowls over and over in somersaults. Its middle legs splay upwards and its rear legs backwards, so that wherever it lands, it lands on feet, though not necessarily right side up. The supple joints take the impact of landing and its claws stabilise the flea on the instant. And there it is, in the midst of cultivation. All this, of course, is not seen with the naked eye. Two developments made it possible to know. A special camera, devised by the Royal Air Force, snapped the flea in mid-bound. And the finding was confirmed by having a flea spring into a frozen fixative, so that, arrested before it expected, it was petrified in the attitude of its leap.

When the flea arrives, not many minutes old, on its first expanse of human skin, instinct draws it to feed. It chooses a convenient spot—a quiet grove amid the tangled flue of a man's legs, likely round the ankle where there is a quick escape in the outlet between sock and trouser; or in the geological folds of a groin. It stands firm, claws rooted. It sets its stiletto drill to the ground and churns the surface cuticle to tenderness. Then in a static dive it raises its tail in the air and drives the sharp proboscis deep. There is a sharp injection of saliva, to prevent the blood coagulating (and which, after a safe interval, will cause the sting and irritation of a day or more). And with the sucking tube securely tapping blood, the flea's gullet dilates and the rich red moisture is sucked upwards. Not, of course, in large quantity. The amount of saliva spurted into the wound has been calculated at 0·0004 of a cubic millimetre; and the possible length of an undisturbed meal suggests a very thin flow of liquid. The engaged flea can sway happily in the enjoyment of its food for hours on end; then, satisfied, stop, lower its abdomen, tug feeding-kit free and return to mat, blanket, or some private nook.

Feeding cannot, in the nature of things, be a regular occurrence. Given the opportunity, and in a warm, dampish atmosphere, the flea will aim to feed every day. In cold weather its appetite diminishes, and it can go weeks between meals. Moreover asceticism lengthens its life. It can, if necessary, fast for up to six months and be none the worse. (And here it is still no match for the laboratory tick which, even with its head cut off to make feeding impossible, survived four abstinent years.) But fasting may induce drowsiness. Signor Bertolotto, whose proud boast it was that 'some of my Fleas have been fed by ladies of distinction', and who had 'sometimes fed twenty on my hand, all feeding at once', noticed that after four days without food his performing fleas were not so proficient at their heavy work. Still, those who are periodically vexed with fleas, and curse at the return of torment weeks after they thought the tormentors were eliminated, may know that the period between was probably passed by the fleas in sleeping off a large and satisfying meal.

For a flea, a meal usually goes before sex. Some bird fleas are known to copulate almost immediately they emerge from the cocoon, without taking a blood meal first. But *Pulex irritans*, in common with most fleas, has a different order of priority. The male needs blood before getting the urge. The female is incapable of ovulating without blood. In the rabbit flea the business is more nicely arranged. Blood alone does not evoke the response. It has to be the blood of a rabbit at a certain stage of pregnancy that gives the idea to resident fleas. Male and female fleas can drill and siphon happily for weeks in close proximity; then, after changes in the rabbit host (described later), they feel suddenly a mutual need, and life, for a while, is all lust and procreation. It is another case of the rabbit flea's superiority over its cousins.

Finding a mate may not be easy for *Pulex irritans*. Quite possibly only a small percentage of his kind ever come to know the brutal transports of sex. All his senses are called into play in the quest. He smells and looks and registers minute currents of air. But the nearest female may be far away, in the antipodes of a waistline, on the far side of a bed, or snoozing in a dustpan. There is a theory—no more than that, and denied categorically by some—that he serenades her with piercing flea music far above the registers known to man. Somehow, if he can, he tracks her down.

A great deal of hokum was talked and thought about the mating of fleas both before and after the invention of the microscope. But though the power of the magnifying lens put the record straight among savants, misconceptions prospered, and still do. Only a few years ago Horace Jakes wrote:

> The male and female flea to you
>   Do not appear distinct;
> But fleas can tell which one is who
>   When maritally linked.

The sexes are, of course, markedly different. For a start the male is generally a good deal smaller than his mate.

In the business of conception, due wonderment must go to the male. He is the sexual marvel of the animal kingdom. He possesses the most elaborate genital armature yet known, and in one case—the jigger flea—he comprises very little but genitalia. He is quite unlike any other male insect. In brief, he possesses two penis rods, curled together like embracing snakes. Inside his body, the smaller of these rods moves outwards lambently, catching the delicate skeins of ready sperm and moving into a groove on the larger longer rod. Then this whole phallic coil slides out from his sensitive rear. The large rod enters the female and guides the thinner along beside it. The thinner continues its passage into the storage organ of the female, and deposits the sperm before retracting. 'Any engin-eer', Miriam Rothschild has written, 'looking objectively at such a fantastically impractical apparatus would bet heavily against its operational success. The astonishing fact is that it works.' There is a picture that shows it working. Two fleas were frozen, suddenly, in embrace and photographed *in flagrante delicto*. Afterwards they were melted back to passion. Without the photograph, much knowledge now possessed would still elude the scientists.

But this is to anticipate. By scent, sight or music, the flea has found his mate.* He approaches her unsteadily, in a demurring zigzag, then pushes his head against hers. She runs forward a little. Smaller than she, he runs beneath her from behind and stands back to belly and tail to tail. He grasps her abdomen with his antennae, and sensuously brushes her parts with a wispy membrane. Then violence comes. His lobster tail curls upward, and with spiny clasps secures a brute-hard genital clutch. His inner workings roll. Rods uncoil, sperm is skimmed, there are pressures and prods, and oily exits and entrances already described. Copulation lasts about

---

* The following description is drawn partly from an article by Dr D. A. Humphries in *Animal Behaviour*, which deals specifically with the Hen Flea, *Ceratophyllus gallinae*. *Pulex irritans*, through scarcity, is less well documented.

three hours, sometimes as long as nine, but stops neither party
from feeding. The male's seed passes, carried by the twin
components of his unwieldy apparatus. He disengages, often
with some difficulty, and moves away. So sharp and indelicate
are the hooks and spines of his organs that the female may in all
likelihood have suffered injury. But she is pregnant, and he is
satisfied, and within hours a new batch of eggs will drop into
the world. This happens repeatedly. Before each clutch arrives
the parents will eat voraciously and defecate with stepped up
rapidity—every four or five minutes instead of every twenty.
So droppings of food will be scattered all over the home area
for the benefit of the larvae. And the blood of humans, after
a passage through the siphons and stomachs of parent fleas,
will be fit to succour their maggot offspring.

Strengthening and growing as a larva, re-forming as a pupa,
reproducing as an adult, fighting and contriving to survive—
the flea's lifework is done. A complex career for an apparently
simple purpose. But so it is with all insects, all animals, and
man included. Birth and death, feeding and mating. For the
flea, the whole cycle may last a month, or a year or more. It
may take in the landscape of a house, a car, a plane, a dog, a
barn, or the intimacies of beggar or princess. Or just a room,
and the cracks in walls, and the brakes and copses of carpet
and bed. For some it may include the laboratory, with forced
feeding, forced starving, frozen copulation, and frosty captivity
in a glass bottle at several degrees below freezing, to be shaken
like coffee beans before a forced thaw brings back feeling to
claw and proboscis. For a diminishing few it can be the con-
scription of show business, slave labour in perpetual harness
under the circus lights, amid the blare of brass bands, under
staring eyes whose pupils alone are the size of fleas.

Fleas have not till recently attracted the persistent attention of
biologists. It will, therefore, be a long time before the dilemmas
of the early evolution of the flea can be resolved. 'Adam Had

'em' runs (in full) what the *Oxford Dictionary of Quotations* calls the shortest English poem—*On the Antiquity of Microbes*. But there is nothing to confirm the poem's contention.

In the absence of fact, there is a deal of myth. According to Danish and Indian legends, fleas were sent by God to punish man for his incorrigible laziness—as spiky, stinging goads to action. Among the Flemish it is told that fleas were created to give women something to do, to force them, presumably, to do the washing when not doing it would have preserved the torments of these insects. An old tale tells of a war of the heavens. Fleas, it was assumed, irritated the wicked as Robin Hood harried the rich; for God had made them specifically to plague the Devil and his agents. But the Devil rallied and created the gnats as anti-missile. Gnats, we are to believe, are the bane of the pious; and the myriad red and itching bumps raised by gnats and fleas are far-flung war-wounds in the struggle between Good and Evil. It is possible to tell a good man from a bad by the irritants he provokes.

The longest account of the origin of fleas was written by that ardent pen-pusher, Willart de Grécourt. The flea appears as a character in several of his sub-Fontaine fables, sub-Voltaire satires and sub-Racine classical dramas, and it is perhaps by way of tribute and gratitude that he turns, towards the end of his life's work, to a sub-erotic poem of some sixteen pages entitled *L'Origine des puces*. The theme is a party of the gods, held in Olympus. Nectar and ambrosia flow freely, and tables creak under piles of sublime meats. With appetite appeased, divine fancy turns amorous. At this point Morpheus, god of slumber, mixes a potion that substitutes a general sleepy listlessness for the orgy that would have been. Cupid is furious, cheated of the supreme tribute to his own powers. '*Qu'un prodige nouveau signale ma puissance*',* he cries, shooting an arrow into the air. The arrow turns itself into a swarm of fleas, hitherto unknown. The insects settle without mercy on all the gods.

* 'Let some new miracle proclaim my power.'

Everyone is being pricked by 'ce peuple sautillant, frétillant, sautant, volant, rampant, grimpant',* and during the efforts to rid them- selves of the little pests the silky dresses of the goddesses suffer 'un grand dérangement'. The stolid clumsiness of the poet is hard to exaggerate. Cupid exhorts his insect force. To a flea, they bite anew, and harder. The gods jump at the assault and when they land male and female are conveniently side by side, disrobed and alert. In moments there are 'mille soupirs pleins de douceur', and the pleasures continue for three full days and as many pages of rheumatic verbiage, during which time the sun, being a god and preoccupied, neither rises nor sets. Prudent Minerva ulti- mately points to the chaos being created among humans, and a halt is called. But the fleas, created as a spur to love, cannot be dispersed until Zeus, feeling at the time crotchety towards humans, descides to banish the insects from Olympus to the mortal world.

There is also a story attributing the origin of fleas to squirrels. It is not a great story, but it is a reminder of how close at times mythology has come to historical truth. Miriam Rothschild has written that the first flea, evolving in a den or burrow, found as its first host a small mammal. Perhaps it was in truth a squirrel.

In the true beginning, it is thought, the flea was not a para- site at all. When the pupa of some species is examined under the microscope, traces of wings, it has been claimed, can be seen on its thorax; from this some entomologists deduce that the ancestor of fleas was a two-winged scavenging insect, related to a forbear of the ordinary fly.

About a hundred million years ago, in what geologists call the Cretaceous age, insects came into their own. It was the great age of the dinosaur, but insects proliferated more than they had before, adapting to new circumstances much faster than other animals. Somewhere and somehow this tiny fly, through the processes of mutation and natural selection, found not only that

* 'this hopping, wriggling, jumping, flying, crawling, climbing race'.

the blood of mammals was palatable and nourishing, but that it was more convenient to make its home in the mammal's nest than fly around in tiresome searching. It was what an aquatic crab might feel about the sea, which can be relied on to stay, as distinct from rock-pools, which come and go. This fly's wings, once it was settled in the cramped quarters of a cave or nest, became a hindrance. Jumping was much more useful. So gradually a species evolved with phenomenally powerful back legs, and the vestigial wings disappeared. This we may call the proto-flea.

We do not know much about the proto-flea, or his successors of the next fifty million years. Even then there is little firm fact in flea prehistory, though interesting relics of the period exist. By this time the world was in the Oligocene age, a time of great climatic warming and abundance of what would now be called tropical vegetation. There were large coniferous forests in the land now covered by the Baltic Sea, in America, and over southern Europe. Sometimes, from individual trees, drops of resin fell square on some unsuspecting insect going about his business. The resin hardened and over subsequent millions of years became what we know as amber.

The unlikeliest avocations possess their quota of mystery and intrigue. When I asked the Custodian of the flea collection at Tring about amber fleas, he seemed to fidget furtively. 'Yes, two of them exist,' he conceded, 'and I know where they are. But I wouldn't like to say much about them.' He paused; around him a vast mausoleum, the classified corpses of over a quarter of a million fleas. 'Early in the century the German owner of one amber flea asked twelve hundred pounds for it. But it's not difficult to manufacture imitation amber fleas. There's a lot of— yes—politics in it.' I have seen amber ants and amber spiders innocently exposed to public gaze in museums. But someone appears to be trying to give amber fleas the sort of international cachet attaching to uranium deposits.*

* *Über die beiden Bernstein—Flöhe* by Professor F. Peus, just published, gives further valuable information on the two amber fleas.

Both the fleas known to be preserved in amber are said to differ little from a certain mole flea of today; it can thus be assumed that forty million years ago fleas had passed through their major evolutionary phases.

What these changes were, and when they took place, is not known. Apart from those vestigial 'wing buds' on the pupa of a few species of flea there is not much certain evidence that they even descended from flying ancestors, certainly not flies. There is a case for proto-beetles being their evolutionary Adams, and another case for proto-scorpion-flies. Nor is anyone clear on what the transitional stages were, or how the flea first became a blood-sucking parasite, or when. Since mammals are the principal victims of the little predators, it is thought that a mammal was the first chosen prey. But a few fleas have been found on snakes and lizards, and although it is likely they were there accidentally, forced to transfer from a mammal recently swallowed, some scientists have thought it possible that fleas first evolved with reptiles as hosts, and have consequently allocated them a few more hundred million years of prehistory. Reptiles have been on the scene a great deal longer than mammals.

Time passed and fleas spread over the world. Insects, small as they are, are often better able to cross seas and mountain ranges than reptiles or even mammals. Certain butterflies migrate under their own power from Britain to the Continent of Europe or vice versa each year. Fleas and others, without the same genetic need, can travel even further, on the back of a migrant bird, concealed on a ship in the hair or fur of a human or some zoo-destined animal, clinging to the back of a wasp or bee, or simply borne away by the wind. It has been calculated that a million insects are present in a column of air one mile square and a thousand feet high. By these and other means, such as the natural dispersal of host animals, the race of fleas transported itself to six continents and established itself firmly on them.

As soon as they settled, fleas began adapting to new conditions. Different species arose, suited to this or that climate, temperature or host. It is true that, compared with other small organisms, they were not outstandingly versatile. There are about three hundred thousand species of beetle at present, over fifteen thousand species of ant and only two thousand of fleas. The trophies for the evolution race, if it is possible to speak of a race between competitors who are not remotely aware of its existence, should probably go to humans, rats and ants. Fleas are far down the list, but they have still shown ingenuity in getting where they are.

One way of seeing how successfully fleas adapted to altered circumstances is to look for a while at their scientific classification. There are in fact several systems, and the standard one, drawn up over twenty years ago, is now in some respects out of date. A new series of large and lengthy tomes is being produced to fill the gap.* But an older, and fairly simple system is a help to understanding the broad variations of different fleas. There are three basic divisions—the mobile fleas, the semi-sedentary fleas, and the sedentary fleas. The first group includes those most commonly encountered by humans in temperate climates—the human, dog, cat, rat, mole and most of the bird fleas. They obviously form the oldest group, since fleas, originally free livers, only got attached to their hosts by stages. These fleas need to settle on their hosts only for feeding, and much of the rest of the time will be spent quietly in nests or ranging freely. But this arrangement has its drawbacks. A host may up and away, and leave the nest deserted for weeks or months. It happens with humans, and more particularly it happens with migrating birds. The chief losers are larval maggots, all of which stay behind when the birds fly away, then change to pupae and adults and find nothing to feed on. There is an enormous wastage because of this mass desertion of large populations. But with most mammal hosts the dangers are not so great.

* Hopkins and Rothschild, *An Illustrated Catalogue of the Rothschild Collection of Fleas in the British Museum.* London.

The second group, the semi-sedentary fleas, afflict only mam-mals. There are none in Britain, some in Europe and plenty in Asia and America. Their chief characteristic is that the females spend most of their adult life on the body of the host, and their appetite for blood, especially when pregnant, is enormous. In this condition the females of a certain species in the category swell in size from about four millimetres to over fifteen. They can cause anaemia and irritation in sheep, and have brought financial losses through infestations of silver-fox farms. Moun-tain sheep of central Asia, when victimised by such fleas—known as alakurts—often find an ally in magpies, which regu-larly pick them out of the wool and eat them.

Third come sedentary fleas, in some ways the most successful, in others the most annoying of all. They divide into two groups, the first of which, stick-fast fleas, clamp their jaws in the skin of the host—usually around the head or neck—throughout their period of ovulation. Their mouthparts are especially developed for this purpose, and the great advantages will become clear when we consider the rabbit flea. The other group of sedentary fleas are known as jiggers,* or chigoes. They are best described shortly, and left to their noxious devices.

Jiggers are found mainly in South America, west and cen-tral Africa and eastern Asia, in all of which their females can menace unshod humans. They seem to have reached their evolutionary pitch in South America, and to have made their way, by Spanish ships, to Africa only as recently as the six-teenth or seventeenth century. They are referred to in an early history of the island of St Domingo, from which a Capuchin friar 'brought away with him from that island a colony of these animals which he permitted to establish themselves in one of his feet; but unfortunately for himself, and for science, the foot intrusted with the precious deposit mortified, was obliged to be

* In America this name is also applied to a parasitic mite otherwise known as the Red Bug.

amputated, and with all its inhabitants committed to the waves'. The same author, Walton, wrote of female slaves in the West Indies being 'frequently employed to extract these pests, which they do with uncommon dexterity'. Earlier this century Albert Schweitzer wrote that at his hospital in tropical Africa it was rare for an African to have ten toes intact. This was due to the jigger.

Science's loss has since been made good, and the life cycle of the common jigger, *Tunga penetrans,* is well known. The female, given a choice, makes her home on the foot of a man, pig, or any other fair-sized mammal. The soft skin between the toes, or under the nails, is regarded by her as an admirable cul-de-sac for the propagation of her species. Using the serrated cutlery of her mouthparts she digs herself inside the skin, then mates *in situ*; settled, she leaves exposed only the tip of her abdomen, through which air passes in, and excreta and eggs out. Gradually, as her eggs grow, she grows, and there develops on the foot a swelling the size of a pea. Eventually, thousands of eggs are ejected. When she dies, her body remains in position. It may cause inflammation or an ulcer, and invites other complications. Many Africans, like the West Indian girls mentioned above, are adept at removing the live flea with the aid of a safety pin. It is often hard to realise that the basic shape of the jigger is identical with that of the irritant more familiar in temperate regions.

Distinguishing one flea species from another by its looks is not always as easy as telling a male from a female by its diminutive size. Apart from some obvious distinctions, identification is the work of the expert; and the layman is in much the same dilemma as the expatriate Chinese to whom most westerners look alike. Differences can be seen, some even without the help of a microscope. But, for the most part, the presence or absence of combs, of eyes, of certain bristles, the structure of the hard outer shell which is the insect equivalent of a skeleton, the shape of the head and mouthparts, and particularly the structure of male and female genitalia—these are the criteria of classification and the clues to the past history of a species. The number of known species has now reached almost to its second thousand, and it increases, on average, by about thirty species discovered each year. 1962 was a bad year, with only nineteen newcomers, but it was an exception.

Fleas, then, have taken different roads at different times, and by trial and error—the stuff of evolution—have modified their parts to suit their surroundings. They are not the cleverest parasites, but they have successfully spread themselves round the world. They are elusive, versatile, insidious. True, if their bite were less irritating—like that of other parasites—they would not have called forth the dazzling array of weapons which has been used against them ever since they made man their table. Even earliest man was able to alter the evolutionary balance immeasurably more than other creatures. Still the achievement of different species in their various ways is remarkable.

One of the commonest fleas encountered by humans is the dog flea. In a random analysis of two thousand fleas collected from humans in England, over half were found to be *Ctenocephalides canis,* for while its natural objectives are dogs and foxes it finds nothing distasteful in man or cats.* Not so the swallow flea which was once starved for nine months, then put on a human arm. It pressed home its siphon, began to suck, then stopped. Examined afterwards is was found not to have let the blood pass as far as its gullet, so disgusting was the taste. Normally, however, a flea will take blood wherever it can. Bat fleas, deprived of bats, will settle on rats without demur, and dog fleas on cats, and hen fleas on pigeons; though they may be prevented—presumably by some tiny deficiency in their new diet—from carrying on all their natural functions.

Cat fleas are another successful species. Unlike the dog flea

* Dog fleas seem to inspire wisdom. 'The dog that is idle barks at his fleas, but he that is hunting feels them not', say the Chinese. A German proverb runs: 'The fatter the flea, the leaner the dog.' There are many others.

and *Pulex irritans* they are found all over the world, not confined to temperate climates. They cause most infestations in
houses and breed fast. However, cats and their fleas have not yet
developed a mutual need. Yet in other species this does happen,
notably the hedgehog flea, *Archaeopsylla erinacei*. Over the millennia hedgehogs seem to have developed an anti-toxin in their
bloodstream to counter the poisonous injections of their fleas.
This refinement has actually left them dependent on fleas.
Twenty years ago F. G. A. M. Smit, Custodian of the Tring
collection, examined two young hedgehogs he found in the
Netherlands. He removed their fleas and counted 828 off one
and 932 off the other. These are exceptional numbers, for usually the hedgehog has no more than fifty or a hundred. The
remarkable thing in this case was that soon after the creatures
had been de-fleaed they died. Presumably, their own anti-toxin,
deprived of toxin to counter, flooded the bloodstream and
killed them.

Hedgehog fleas are supposed by some to have a special verti-
cal jump, but I have not found the scientist who confirms it.
The reason given for the jump is that hedgehogs are creatures of
unchanging habit. Like badgers, they cover precisely the same
route time and time again. If a flea falls off it is said to wait
awhile and then start jumping straight up into the air. Sooner
or later the hedgehog, true to custom, will return along the
same route, and before long one of the jumps will land the flea
back on the body from which it fell. It is a story that had a
strong currency fifty years ago and was reported in many books.
It probably started as a joke. Another popular misconception is
that monkeys search each other for fleas, which in fact seldom
afflict them. What they are looking for are little bits of scurf, for
they enjoy its taste.

The biggest flea in the world is the North American *His-
trichopsylla schefferi,* which measures slightly over a quarter of an
inch. In Britain the largest species is a mole and vole flea *His-
trichopsylla talpae* talpae, normally a little over half the length

of *H. schefferi*. Oddly, this largest British flea infests—as well as the mole, vole and wood-mouse—the smallest mammal, the pygmy shrew. Not long ago a mole flea of record size—a quarter of an inch—was removed from a shrew, and caused its discov- erers to wonder if it had not been an exceptional nuisance. Measure for measure, a parasite of similar size on a man would be no smaller than a rat, crawling and sucking at will over the limited expanses of the human person. It was indeed an old- time torture, to trap a rat inside an inverted bowl on a man's belly. Such torment is the shrew's daily lot, but it copes.

Perhaps the most distinguished species and, like the jigger, a specialist with a quite remarkable way of life, is the European rabbit flea (*Spilopsyllus cuniculi* Dale). It is a sedentary species, found most commonly in the spring, clustered round the ears of rabbits whence it is least likely to be ejected by the host. Most rabbits suffer from fleas, and a normal community found on any one animal would number seventy or so. Sometimes a cat that successfully goes out rabbiting will catch a rabbit flea, and for a while its new acquisition will cling to its ear or neck. But rabbit fleas cannot long survive without rabbits, and men are seldom if ever bothered by them. There is an irony here. The rabbit flea has adapted itself to its host by the most sophisticated evolutionary process and has made itself as a result a much more successful breeder than, say, the rat flea. But it has at the same time evolved exclusive dependancy on the rabbit. If its rabbit dies, and there are no more nearby, the flea dies soon afterwards. If a pandemic disease, like myxomatosis, spreads, and kills—as it did in Britain—a hundred million rabbits, then something like seventy times that number of fleas succumb, and possibly as many as ten thousand million. Not so with the rat flea or many others which, lacking a special link with their hosts, can go over to another camp. The rat flea has this much in common with the rat, that it can leave a sinking vessel and live to tell the tale.

On balance the rabbit flea's close involvement with the

rabbit has been a distinct benefit to it.* The essence of this re-
lationship is that in the course of a hundred million years or so
it has given over to the rabbit full control of its own breeding
cycle. No female rabbit flea can ever breed unless it has settled
on a female rabbit and that rabbit has, herself, become pregnant. When this happens the hormone content of the rabbit's
blood begins to change. Then, approximately ten days before
the rabbit bears her young, the state of her hormones causes the
flea itself to begin ovulating. On the last day of the rabbit's
pregnancy the flea's eggs are ripe, and ready to be fertilised.
Young rabbits are born; and within a few hours the female
fleas have detached themselves from the doe's ears, and jumped
on to the young. Now they start feeding again, and once again
the quality of the host's blood is a cue for further action. After a
meal of the young rabbit's blood the female flea suddenly becomes sexually attractive. For weeks beforehand males and
females have all cohabited on the ear of a rabbit without any
apparent awareness of each other's sexuality. Now, in their new
infantile surroundings they leap into action and mate busily.
Egg-laying follows, spaced over several days. Thus the larvae,
as soon as they emerge, have two marked benefits over their less
advanced cousins. The floor of the particular part of the warren
in which they find themselves is well supplied with rabbit
blood in the form of a profusion of parental droppings. And
there before them are the young rabbits who will in the course of
time become their own adopted hosts.

Examples of skilful adapting are seen among the whole
group of bird fleas, which were able, comparatively late in their
history, to make the big jump from life in the damp burrows of

---

* The Hon. Miriam Rothschild has carried out momentous research on this
involvement, besides other aspects of parasites, and I have drawn this account
from papers published by her. She is a dedicated amateur, and has passed no
public examinations, though Oxford made her an Honorary Doctor of Science
in 1968. 'She takes a perverse pleasure', her daughter has written, 'in keeping
livestock in the bathroom.'

mammals to the dry and airy nests of birds. Some learned to cope with the annual migrations of their hosts by something resembling hibernation; they wake and assemble in actual swarms at the entrances of nests or—in the case of sand-martins —burrows, at the very time of their host's return from Africa or the South Pacific, like the staff in some manorial household come out to greet their beneficent master. Some—like the stick- tight hen flea—have sacrificed the once-prized power of jump- ing in order to cling round the eyes or wattles of their poultry landlords, out of reach of the most conscientious preening.

Fleas' fleas

Hobbes clearly proves that every creature
Lives in a state of war, by nature:
So, naturalists observe, a flea
Hath smaller fleas that on him prey;
And these have smaller fleas to bite 'em,
And so proceed *ad infinitum*.
Thus every poet, in his kind,
Is bit by him that comes behind.

Hobbes had died half a century before Dean Swift wrote those lines. A little after Hobbes, Antoni van Leeuwenhoek pio- neered the use of the microscope and found that fleas suffered from parasites themselves, that as a group they get quite as good as they give. The news came to Swift's ears and inspired him to verse. So fleas gave birth to another literary tradition. This one continued through the pen of a Victorian mathematician, Augustus de Morgan—

Great fleas have little fleas upon their backs to bite 'em,
And little fleas have lesser fleas, and so *ad infinitum*.
And the great fleas themselves, in turn, have greater fleas to go on;
While these in turn have greater still, and greater still, and so on.

Earlier this century Hans Zinssner, forsaking the flea but not
the concept in his *Rats, Lice and History*, wrote that 'the plant
does the work with its roots and green leaves. The cow eats the
plant. Man eats both of them, and bacteria (or investment
bankers) eat the man. . . . In the last analysis man may be
defined as a parasite on a vegetable.' Don Marquis, insect-
loving author of *archy and mehitabel*, later reinstated fleas with a
free verse version of Swift's lines.

Science, however, is the language of fact and no flea was ever
fed on by another. The parasites of fleas are creatures of altogether different character. There are nematode worms, related to
the hookworm, which insinuate themselves into the reproductive organs of a flea, eat away until they have castrated it and
then, if it dies, desert it for another. There are a number of protozoan parasites that feed on other internal parts of the flea.
Tapeworms can pass an early stage in a flea before passing to
dog or human. The most common kind of flea parasite is the
mite. Various species of mite enjoy the flea at various stages of
its development. Some lay their eggs *in* the larvae of the flea; as
soon as they emerge the mite larvae eat their way out of the flea-
maggot and kill it in the process. Others feed on the pupa,
slowly devouring the helpless, mummified body. Others again
live on the full-grown flea, half under the flanges of its segments,
and use the flea's leap for their own migration. As many as 150
have been found on a single flea.

Minuter still, in a steady progression *ad infinitum*, various bacteria and bacilli infect fleas, sometimes harming them, sometimes innocuous. Most virulent is the plague bacillus, deadly
without distinction to rat, flea and man. Numbers of these
organisms block the flea's gut, and so starve it.

Nor are a flea's hazards confined to creatures as small to it as
it is to man. It lives a life of macrocosmic hostility too. Most
dangerous of its larger menaces is usually its host's defences—
the cutting grip of men's finger-nails, or the rampaging beak of
a meticulous bird. During love-play buck rabbits often de-flea

their mates. A laboratory mouse was once invested with fifty mouse fleas and after a week there were only fourteen survivors, the rest having succumbed to the mouse's cleansing, combing teeth. Digested fleas are found in the crops of birds. There are insects (other than hosts) which thrive on a meal of fleas. So, in birds' nests, certain kinds of beetle devour the creatures in large numbers; and ants have been known to make a meal of them too. If a flea bites the hand that feeds it, it often suffers a punish-ment to suit the crime.

9

THE TWENTIETH-CENTURY
FLEA

The great tragedy of Science—the slaying of a beautiful hypothesis
by an ugly fact.   T. H. HUXLEY

It was the work of this century to fill in the details of fleas' lives
and the flea world. No period ever gave the flea so much attention as the aftermath of the Indian plague. From the beginning
of man's time this insect had bothered and fascinated him. But
it never preoccupied him till it was thought to kill. Then the
work really began. Even so, fleas had a long way to catch up
on less scabrous insects—ants and bees and butterflies. True,
Rothschild and others were able to send the number of known
species up from seventy to four hundred in two decades. Yet
fifty years later, when we know it is nearing two thousand, it is
still rising. A recent complaint shows how the work has proceeded since those pioneer days. 'A mere thousand works on
fleas have been published in the last five years', wrote Miriam
Rothschild, daughter of Nathaniel Charles, in 1965. Her
father would have been delighted at a tenth the number.

The life has gone out of poetic fleas, and of moral and immoral and reverend and music-hall fleas. Slum clearance has
almost buried the performing flea. Baths and vacuum cleaners
and DDT, in much of the western world, have wrought geno-
cide on the everyday irritant flea. None of us scratch as much as
our parents. Dogs, cats, rats and birds maintain their own
quota, but the faithful and affectionate creature that clung to a
man wherever he went is going the way of the great auk, the
dodo and the pterodactyl.

For our purposes the twentieth-century flea is a clean-cut creature, a familiar of laboratories, checked, watched and regulated. In the great flea centres of the world—Tring, Washington, Stavropol in Russia—he has been classified and reclassified, diagnosed and dissected, peered at and tabulated. We have seen him frozen stiff in compromising poses, or in mid-air leaps. For nine months he has been kept below zero in a refrigerator. Russians, Canadians, Americans and Englishmen have scrutinised each instant of his sex-life, and reduced the miraculous machinery that brings it about to the two dimensions of scholarly pages. Californians have made him radioactive, to track his movements. Biology graduates reflect for days on what new aspect of flea genetics, flea distribution, flea allergies, or fleabites they can cover in their projected flea theses.

Not, it must be said, without cause. Allowed to go free, fleas are a potential menace as much as ever they used to be. Plague is no more resolved than other mass-killing maladies. It remains dormant over much of the world, and it could surprise the world as much as homely 'flu did when it raised itself to the status of an apocalyptic spectre. Right across Asia, from Turkey to Mongolia, plague still seethes among the rodent population. In southern Africa it lurks endemic in the multimammate mouse. Parts of the western United States are rife with it, for it was endemic in the waterside rat there, eliminated this species and passed for subsistence to the squirrel. It seldom reaches man. But not long ago in California it passed among a colony of prairie dogs who were unable to live with it like the squirrels. It killed three hundred. Fleas were responsible, and in Vietnam they are bringing it once more to man.

In big towns rats are the chief menace. If plague came to them fleas might bring it to us. And it might come, imported at the tail end of a weird ecology. Asian gerbils go through one of their periodic and unaccountable population explosions. They are brought closer in touch with country rats of farm areas. Fleas pass on the plague. They pass it from country rats to town rats, and it reaches docks and ships. It travels by sea and one day, conceivably, the rats of London, Paris and New York have it, and begin to die in numbers. Choking fleas jump from their cooling bodies to a tramp, a camper, a sewage worker, and within days an ancestral instinct in man is cowering at the mention of plague; and the sweat, the buboes and the climate of panic are lording it over the population. Camus' plague took place in Oran, Algeria, in the 1940's. He made up the story, but scientists who read it marvel at its plausibility.

Kill off rats, or rat fleas, or both, is the answer. Neither is easily done. In India they sprinkle a box with DDT and put meat inside it and leave it for the rats. A rat takes the meat and is flecked with the insecticide, which it spreads around the nest as soon as it gets home. But it is a laborious, fallible and expensive way of eliminating one nest fleas. Rats themselves are as big a problem. Female rats breed at three months old and can produce a litter of ten or more every six weeks through the year. Rats are depressingly sly about taking poison, and some are now immune to Warfarin, a poison used over the world since 1950.

In Paris every fifteen years or so rat numbers multiply. Many leave the thousand miles of city sewers and in their exodus are forced to jostle through parts of the city. Gendarmes fight them back with batons and capes. At present the transference of *Les Halles*, the food market, outside Paris is going to leave a vast surplus of starving rats in the city.

Rats are still with us in plenty. So too are their fleas. There is no certain reason for our long immunity from plague. It may be better ships and more hygienic holds, or the greased hawsers that keep rats out of them, or new-style granaries proof against rats, or the reliable vaccine that has been used on millions, or any number of traps, checks and contraptions that the ingenuity of science has evolved. But nobody knows for sure, and while nobody knows the threat may be present.

Plague is not the only hazard for fleas, though it is one of tenderest concern to men. With other parasites they share both guilt and destruction in the transference of typhoid, tularaemia, and a number of other diseases. But in one cataclysmic case they spread a killing disease in the service of man.

Rabbits in South America have lived with and been immune to the virus of myxomatosis for possibly centuries. In 1898 some European rabbits, of a species new to the area, were introduced to Uruguay and promptly fell victim to it. In the first half of this century it spread a little into the western United States, killing those rabbits which had not learned to live with it. In the late 'forties it was introduced to Australia in a purposeful attempt to cut down the ravages of rabbits. Millions eventually died. In this case the main carrier was the mosquito, but in their bad seasons fleas took over distribution. In 1952 myxomatosis was introduced into France. A year later it came to England. Here the European rabbit flea was the main vector, and did its work thoroughly. An estimated hundred million rabbits died in Britain. But again the flea was sacrifice as well as agent. Each rabbit would carry a community of as much as seventy-five fleas, and most of these would die. The depradations on the rabbit flea world were uncountable.

Death and disease are the contemporary themes of the flea. There is a little to redeem it. The liquid it injects in bites, for instance, could be used to prevent thrombosis, being a powerful anti-coagulant. Yet there is more to toll the flea's menace. In Russia, America and Britain the main research goes on. But in each country some continues behind locked doors. There is little point in speculating, but the Russians, with their Anti-Plague Research Institutes, the Americans with their Microbiological Institutes, seem—even considering the threatening horrors of the blight—to stint not at all in their work on the flea. It could be simply a thorough scrutiny to prevent new plague outbreaks. But national expenditures on so lavish a scale often suggest more positive aims.

There is secrecy too around the British Microbiological Research Establishment, where they research on fleas. In 1962 forty-four-year-old Geoffrey Bacon, a worker there, died; and was found to have died of the germ of pneumonic plague. Has the flea a greater part still to play in the course of human history? Will it be instrumental at the end?

Death, disease and gloomy prognoses. Till the scientists came the flea played many parts, and we hated it but had to laugh at it, and used it for our tales, proverbs and poems. Then we busied ourselves with its darker habits and by doing so opened a Pandora's Box of death and destruction, casting away frivolity and amusement. Now, we may have to look on the flea as an enemy. Already, what some scientists do on the grand scale we repeat with our flits and aerosol containers. It is war, and perhaps war to the end of both kinds.

And what of the flea? He had reason enough in sixty years to look on men through different eyes, to tire of his role as an irking, pricking, irreverent court fool. Like the savage subjected to western ways one day and hanged the next for a ritual murder to appease his gods, he has no love for the advances of civilisation. No flea ever knowingly killed a man. The deaths he brought spelt his own death from the same cause. And now he is an outcast from men's houses, an object for laboratories. The great lover of the fold and cranny is exposed to the lights of academic scrutiny.

Where the old instincts linger, where he is born with a zeal for man and tries to live with man he is courting execution. Sooner or later, looking up from vest, jacket, blanket or cupboard crack he will see and feel the quick descent of that ominous white powder, to him a cloud that screens off his world. After the deluge of an instant his segments and legs and proboscis will be clogged with the gummy grains; and a gaseous vapour will clog his breathing pores. Then heat, an auto-da-fé in petrol. He will jump from powder into powder and every move will clam his joints the more. White powder, white heat.

It will scar his shell but burn his entrails. And very quickly he will be dead, an empty carcase with little appeal even for his own kinds of parasite. And the puffing out of his speck of life will again lift the balance of nature infinitesimally, as man commands it should be lifted. For the days that are left are with the race of man, however many there may be left of those.

PREVENTION AND CURE

An Englishman will burn a bed to catch a flea.

TURKISH PROVERB

Until now, I think, no-one has been impelled by the biting of
fleas to write a book, though some have turned to verse as a vent
for frustration. Others wriggle in fettered fury and a few go mad.
The remarkable thing is that not everyone regards the spot as
one of bother. Where fleas bite, wrote Moufet, 'they leave a red
spot as a Trophie of their force'. And whereas some chafe at the
memorial as the Irish at their erstwhile Nelson statue, others
ignore it entirely. '*Quant à moi*', declared a Frenchwoman, '*ce
n'est pas la morsure, c'est la promenade.*' She resented not the bite
but the creepy itching that recorded the flea's progress over her
skin.

Researchers—and there is much research on the matter—
find that after the first few bites some people develop an immunity, some are immune by nature, while for others the bites
are anaphylactic. That is, instead of providing immunity they
increase the susceptibility of the victim. Even the marks left
vary considerably. Some are barely visible. Others grow into
papules which irritate pungently for up to a week. They appear
to affect the young more than the old, and are said—though it is
arguable—to punish women more than men. Age, sex, smell
(not of a kind distinguished by human nostrils), and fleshiness
appear to be factors governing fleas' choice.

Karl von Frisch, a popular German entomologist, once
shared a hotel room with a friend in Naples. The two men were
attending a conference in the town. Fleas infested the room, and
each evening before going to bed both scholars paraded in

nightgown ritual up and down the room, attracting latent fleas. Then they swiftly stripped, caught and counted. Von Frisch's average was a bag of five, his friend's thirty or forty. The friend was obviously more magnetic. Nevertheless it was von Frisch who suffered most. Each of his bites became a large red blister. His friend's could hardly be seen.

Itching and disease are not the only problems. The results of known allergies to bites can be quite as disturbing as psycho- logical obsession. (Researchers here experience the same prob- lem as flea-circus owners—scarcity of fleas; and though the scarcity itself is a mark of the diminution of suffering, it is not helpful to those many still affected.) Given, then, the various allergies, neuroses and other torments, a few practical words on the repulsion of the beast and the cure of its bite would not be out of place.

Where the problem of fleas becomes a national interest, as through plague or other disease, killing must be on the scale of warfare. To this end rodent-killers, sprays, gases, poisons and ubiquitous DDT all play their part. In parts of Asia their cost becomes an appreciable part of the national budget. In the West, however, nothing has been more effective than the in- struments of personal and domestic hygiene used on a national scale.

Within living memory floors and furniture were wiped with wet cloths to keep them clean. This gave the brood of flea larvae the moisture they required and so spread the species. Then came dry methods of cleaning, notably the vacuum cleaner. This, combined with central heating, hot water pipes, and gas and electric fires, helped to expel fleas. The spread of baths down the social scale, and more frequent changing into clean clothes, hindered the life cycle of the insect and virtually banished the human flea from most homes. Twenty years ago newspapers commonly reported a cyclic blight in the population of fleas. It was the only way they could explain the gradual drop in num- bers of the vermin. But they were wrong. Fleas were being

ousted by the methodical spread of defences against them—
cleaners, polishes and soap.

Still many people suffer. Dogs and cats bring in their
troubles and pass them on, in an aggressively physical sense.
There are three remedies—to repel fleas, to eliminate them in-
directly, and to catch and execute them.

Some of the old repellent ways mentioned elsewhere are valid
still, but the modern age is right to appeal to science instead
of time-honoured, time-consuming convention. Iodoform, a
crystalline compound of iodine, is one of science's answers.
Benzyl benzoate and dimethyl phthalate, and paraffin oils
applied to clothes, perform the same repelling function. Socks,
trouser-ends, cuffs and collars are the parts that need attention
most. All these repellents are obtained from chemists, under
more simple proprietary names.

Elimination is a surer method. DDT is the most familiar
pulicide, and although resistance is growing in the insect world,
it remains effective for general use. Patented insecticides in
powder form, dusted on dogs and cats, kill two birds—to use a
metaphor of nature—by relieving the animal and saving the
human on whom the flea might spring. Advice should be
taken on insecticides suitable for cats since they lick themselves
a lot. When a room or house becomes infested it can be dealt
with by washing the floors and any wooden cracks with hot
soap-suds, or spreading all cracks with naphthaline, then
closing all doors for a few hours. If this fails fumigation is
necessary. Flake naphthaline is used for this—five pounds per
thousand cubic feet—but it is best done professionally. It requires vacating the affected space for about a day, and thorough
cleaning thereafter.

These are extreme and thorough methods. More often than
not there is a simple need to catch a flea, trespassing across a
body. Seen, it should be seized. Those able to should crack it
to extinction between the nails of thumb and forefinger. However, both seizing and cracking are tricky operations. A flea,

moreover, may be felt and not seen. If felt clearly, and easily located, it can be clamped by the pressure of fingers over the clothes that conceal it. Privacy is necessary for what follows, the spectacle being both absurd and indecent. A disabled undress‑ ing takes place by means of the hand still free. This done, the clamp hand, maintaining pressure on that area where the flea is assumed to be, folds into its hold the surrounding inches of cloth, so imprisoning the flea in a pocket of fabric. This cluster is then swiftly whisked over a sink or bath, then released and shaken. The flea should fall out, and does so about once in seven instances. It is often useful to have soap, vaseline or other lubricant at hand to trap the offender. Some people, failing to locate the flea precisely, prefer to undress standing in a bath. They then shake and turn inside out each garment as it comes off. None of these methods is foolproof. All, consequently, have some of the suspense of the chase.

If all fails, the flea will surely bite. Relief, for those who suffer most, is not easily found. Alternative sources of relief are found in (not to mince words) an alcoholic solution of menthol, car‑ bolated vaseline, mepyramine maleate cream or antihistamine cream. These anodyne lotions, again, are sold under different names. The advantage of the scientific description is that it is understood by chemists everywhere. Individuals respond to different treatments in different ways. Experiment may be needed. Those who still suffer may take a lesson from those dogs which, wanting to be alone, turn their backs on company; and try to believe they are not tickled at all.

ACKNOWLEDGMENTS

Mrs. H. M. Davies, Jonathan Cape Ltd. and Wesleyan University Press for permission to quote the last verse of 'The Hunt' from *The Complete Poems of W. H. Davies*.

Sir Alan Herbert and Methuen & Co. Ltd. for permission to quote Sir Alan Herbert's poem 'The Flea'.

Hamish Hamilton Ltd. and Alfred A. Knopf, Inc., for permission to quote from *The Plague* by Albert Camus, translated by Stuart Gilbert: Hamish Hamilton Ltd., London, 1948, and Alfred A. Knopf, New York, 1948.

INDEX

Aesop, 27, 39, 40–42
Africa, 31, 102, 112
Aitutaki, 36
Andersen, Hans Christian, 42–43, 92
Antihistamine cream, 120
Ants, 6, 101, 110
Arabs, 9, 77
Archy and Mehitabel, 109
Aristophanes, 91
Aristotle, 66
Australia, 82, 114
Autobiography of a Flea, 50–51

Bacon, Francis, 66
Bacon, Geoffrey, 115
Bacon, Roger, 66
Bacteriological warfare, 114
Badgers, 9
Banks, Sir Joseph, 17, 18, 85
Beaumont and Fletcher, 15
Becket, Thomas à, 12
Bedbugs, 6, 7, 8, 33
Beetles, 101, 110
Belch, Sir Toby, 13
Bellarmine, Cardinal, 12
Bellevue Park, Manchester, 62–63
Belloc, Hilaire, 24
Benzyl benzoate, 119
Bertolotto, L., 35, 58, 59, 60, 61, 62, 63, 64, 85, 86, 89, 93
Bible, 11
Black death, 76
Blake, William, 19–22
Bohemia, 22
Bristowe, W. S., 13
British Microbiological Research Establishment, 115
British Museum, 49
Bugs, 8

Bunyan, John, 39
Burton, Richard, 10
Byzantium, 75–76

Calabria, 25
California, 112
Camel, 41–42
Camus, Albert, 73, 74, 113
Carroll, Lewis, 9, 39
Catherine the Great, 80
Celsus, 28
Celts, 39
Cestone, Iacinto, 68–69
Chaliapin, 11
Chaucer, 13
China, 80
Cholera, 71
Christina, Queen, 57
Clark, 10
Cowper, William, 18
'Crab', 7
Cretaceous age, 98
Crimea, 76

Dark Ages, 11
Davies, W. H., 33
David, 11
DDT, 111, 113, 119
Desroches family, 44–45, 46
Dimethyl phthalate, 119
Diphtheria, 71
Disraeli, Benjamin, 19
Donne, Jack, 56
Donne, John, 15, 16, 46–47
Douglas, Norman, 24–25
Dublin, 1

Edinburgh Museum of Childhood, 57

123

INDEX